Developing Knowledge & Skills for Child & Family Social Work

Sara Miller McCune founded SAGE Publishing in 1965 to support the dissemination of usable knowledge and educate a global community. SAGE publishes more than 1,000 journals and over 800 new books each year, spanning a wide range of subject areas. Our growing selection of library products includes archives, data, case studies and video. SAGE remains majority owned by our founder and after her lifetime will become owned by a charitable trust that secures the company's continued independence.

Los Angeles | London | New Delhi | Singapore | Washington DC | Melbourne

Developing Knowledge & Skills for Child & Family Social Work

Barry Fearnley

Learning Matters
A SAGE Publishing Company
1 Oliver's Yard
55 City Road
London EC1Y 1SP

SAGE Publications Inc.
2455 Teller Road
Thousand Oaks, California 91320

SAGE Publications India Pvt Ltd
B 1/I 1 Mohan Cooperative Industrial Area
Mathura Road
New Delhi 110 044

SAGE Publications Asia-Pacific Pte Ltd
3 Church Street
#10-04 Samsung Hub
Singapore 049483

Library of Congress Control Number: 2021949946

British Library Cataloguing in Publication Data

A catalogue record for this book is available from the British Library

Editor: Kate Keers
Development editor: Sarah Turpie
Senior project editor: Chris Marke
Marketing manager: Camille Richmond
Project management: TNQ Technologies
Cover design: Wendy Scott
Typeset by: TNQ Technologies

ISBN 978-1-5297-6307-2
ISBN 978-1-5297-6306-5 (pbk)

Contents

Since launching in 2003, *Transforming Social Work Practice* has become the market-leading series for social work students. Each book is:

- Affordable
- Written to the Professional Capabilities Framework
- Mapped to the Social Work curriculum
- Practical with clear links between theory and practice

These books use activities and case studies to build critical thinking and reflection skills and will help social work students to develop good practice through learning.

BESTSELLING TEXTBOOKS

7th Edition
Social Work & Mental Health
Malcolm Golightley & Robert Goemans

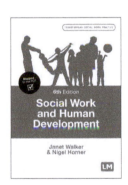

6th Edition
Social Work and Human Development
Janet Walker & Nigel Horner

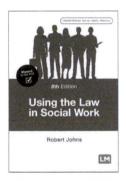

8th Edition
Using the Law in Social Work
Robert Johns

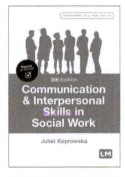

5th Edition
Communication & Interpersonal Skills in Social Work
Juliet Koprowska

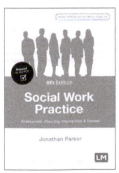

6th Edition
Social Work Practice
Assessment, Planning, Intervention & Review
Jonathan Parker

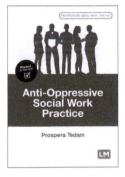

Anti-Oppressive Social Work Practice
Prospera Tedam

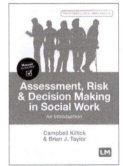

Assessment, Risk & Decision Making in Social Work
An Introduction
Campbell Killick & Brian J. Taylor

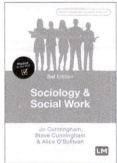

3rd Edition
Sociology & Social Work
Jo Cunningham, Steve Cunningham & Alice O'Sullivan

About the Series Editor

DR JONATHAN PARKER is Professor of Society & Social Welfare at Bournemouth University. He has published widely on social work education, policy, theory for practice, disadvantage, marginalization and violence, across the world.

About the author

Barry Fearnley is a social worker with over 20 years experience working with children and families. He is currently working for a university as a Coach – Child and Adult Workforce. His previous experience includes Head of Partnerships Social Work and Social Care, senior lecturer and a children and families social worker. He has been a practice educator for social work students in both children and families and adult services. He has supported newly qualified social workers undertaking their Assessed and Supported Year in Employment (ASYE) and social workers in their continual professional development. His PhD explored the everyday experiences of young women who are also mothers.

List of abbreviations

ASYE—Assessed and Supported Year in Employment
BASW—British Association of Social Workers
CAMHS—Child and Adolescent Mental Health Services
CEOP—Child Exploitation and Online Protection Centre
CSE—Child Sexual Exploitation
GDPR—General Data Protection Regulation
GIRFEC—Getting It Right for Every Child
IFSW—International Association Federation of Social Workers
IPV—Intimate Partner Violence
KSS—Knowledge and Skills Statement for Child and Family Practitioners
MARAC—Multi-Agency Risk Assessment Conference
MASH—Multi-Agency Safeguarding Hub
NEET—Not in Education, Employment or Training
NQSW—Newly Qualified Social Worker
NSPCC—National Society for the Prevention of Cruelty to Children
PCF—Professional Capabilities Framework
PIES—Physical – Intellectual – Emotional – Social (aspects of child development)
PPCT—Process-Person-Context-Time
QAA—Quality Assurance Agency
SCR—Serious Case Review
SEND—Special Educational Needs and Disabilities
SSSC—Scottish Social Services Council
SWE—Social Work England
UC—Universal Credit
UN—United Nations
UK—United Kingdom

Series editor's preface

The rapid and continual changes permeating our contemporary world appear unabated as the UK moves from a complex and messy withdrawal from the European Union towards unknown futures and from a global pandemic that illuminates the need for cooperation, forging relationships and promoting intergenerational alliances. These events, alongside increasing awareness of the climate emergency facing us all, but exacting a greater toll on people experiencing poverty, disadvantage and marginalisation in our societies, demonstrate the importance of social work for citizen's rights. It is into this febrile context that you come as social work students and to which you have the potential to offer so much.

Values and ethics lie at the heart of social work practice, and so figure highly within social work education, and we address these throughout all the books in the series. The positions that we take in terms of values and ethics is, to an extent, determined by context, time and experience, and these are expressed in different ways by students coming into social work education today. For those of you considering working in the area of children and families, your values will guide, enervate and drive your practice, and it will be important to reflect continually on your own experiences as a child and young person and what you bring from that to your social work role.

Since the turn of this century we have witnessed shifts and challenges as the marketised neoliberal landscape of politics, economy and social life may attract little comment or contest from some. We have observed the political machinery directing much of statutory social work towards a focus on individuals apart from their environment. However, we have also seen a new turn to the social in the #MeToo campaign where unquestioned entitlement to women's bodies and psychology is exposed and resisted. We have seen defiance of those perpetuating social injustices that see long-term migrants alongside today's migrants abused and shunned by society, institutions as well as individuals. Questioning the status quo in social and public policy assumed greater significance during the COVID-19 pandemic in which damage to health and social care wrought by over 10 years of austerity measures were clearly exposed. We stand at a time in which social policy and the well-being of others are seen as priorities, and the work of social workers is recognised as a key service.

It is likely that, as a student of social work, you will lay bare and face many previously unquestioned assumptions, which can be very perplexing and uncover needs for learning, support and understanding. This series of books acts as an aid as you make these steps. Each book stands in a long and international tradition of social work that promotes social justice and human rights, introducing you to the importance of sometimes new and difficult concepts, and inculcating the importance of close questioning of yourself as you make your journey towards becoming part of that tradition. It encourages you also to consider your own position and experiences, the fields you inhabit, the systems of which you are part and the dispositions, or *habitus*, that guide you. This book will help you understand yourself and those with whom you work, drawing on this rich theoretical underpinning.

There are numerous contemporary challenges for the wider world, and for all four countries of the UK. These include political shifts to the 'popular' Right, a growing antipathy to care and support, and dealing with lies and 'alternative truths' in our daily lives, which, unfortunately, increase the lack of trust people have in the societal institutions that are there to help support them. Alongside this is the need to address the impact of an increasingly ageing population with its attendant social care needs and working with the financial implications that such a changing demography brings. Working intergenerationally is, of course, central to a whole family approach of which children and families social work is part. At the other end of the lifespan to older people, the need for high-quality childcare, welfare and safeguarding services has been highlighted as society develops and responds to the changing complexion. This is the focus of this book. As demand rises so do the costs and the unquestioned assumption that austerity measures are necessary continues to create tensions and restrictions in services, policies and expectations.

As a social worker you will work with a diverse range of people throughout your career, many of whom have experienced significant, even traumatic, events that require a professional and caring response. As well as working with individuals, however, you may be required to respond to the needs of a particular community disadvantaged by local, national or world events or groups excluded within their local communities because of assumptions made about them.

The importance of high-quality social work education remains if we are to adequately address the complexities of modern life whether those be of individuals, families, groups or communities. We should continually strive for excellence in education as this allows us to focus clearly on what knowledge is useful to engage with when learning to be a social worker. Questioning everything, especially from a position of knowledge, is central to being a social worker.

The books in this series respond to the agendas driven by changes brought about by professional bodies, governments and disciplinary reviews. They aim to build on and offer introductory texts based on up-to-date knowledge and to help communicate this in an accessible way, so preparing the ground for future study and for encouraging good practice as you develop your social work career. Each book is written by someone passionate about social work and social services and aims to instil that passion in others.

Social workers engage in constant communication using a wide array of media to do so. Barry Fearnley's book immerses you into the professional practice of social work with children and families. This is something each and everyone reading the book has experience of, albeit in many different and varied ways. The book takes an important theoretical approach drawing on ecosystemic models that have served social workers well for many years in understanding the living contexts in which children and young people love and grow. Fearnley brings passion and erudition to childcare social work in a way which will instil in you a deep desire to work alongside children, young people and their families and others to effect positive change and to claim the futures they so richly deserve.

Professor Jonathan Parker

October 2021

Introduction

This book is about developing the knowledge and skills required for child and family social work. It is an introductory text primarily aimed at students starting their journey to becoming a social worker. Whether undergraduate, postgraduate or employment-based apprenticeship route, this book will be useful for the beginning of your studies and for subsequent years as you progress into professional practice. The book will also be of value to practice educators, practice supervisors and all those who support students on placement and within a work-based context. Furthermore, this book should appeal to people considering a career in social work or working with young people. It will also assist students undertaking social, health and education related courses in further and higher education. Additionally, nurses, midwives, health visitors, pastoral support and allied professionals will develop knowledge and skills in relation to working with children and families.

Throughout the book importance will be placed on integrating contemporary social work practice with theoretical concepts, different approaches and tools. Additionally, there will be an emphasis on critical reflection including reflecting on practice as well as preparing for practice. Diagrams, activities, case studies and research information have been included to develop your learning and development. Further reading has been included at the end of each chapter to enable you to develop your knowledge and gain a greater understanding of working with children, young people and families.

Requirements for social work education

Social work education in the United Kingdom (UK) has undergone a major transformation to ensure that students develop the knowledge, skills, values and ethics required to become a social worker. Qualified social workers are educated to at least honours degree level. Social work is a profession that is practised all over the world working in complex, demanding and uncertain environments. The following global definition of the social work profession was approved by the International Association of Schools of Social Work and International Federation of Social Workers (IFSW) in July 2014:

Social work is a practice-based profession and an academic discipline that promotes social change and development, social cohesion, and the empowerment and liberation of people. Principles of social justice, human rights, collective responsibility and respect for diversities are central to social work. Underpinned by theories of social work, social sciences, humanities and indigenous knowledges, social work engages people and structures to address life challenges and enhance wellbeing. The above definition may be amplified at national and/or regional levels.

(IFSW, 2014)

This definition illustrates the importance of promoting social change, empowerment, respect for diversities, working with individuals, enhancing well-being and challenging structures, which are all key aspects of the social work role. We will also consider the UK's four nation's Professional Standards along with the Professional Capabilities Framework (PCF) and Knowledge and Skills Statement for Child and Family Practitioners (KSS), all of which align with the above definition. This book will meet the PCF for social work; Appendix 1 provides an overview of the Framework, and also refers to the KSS and Professional Standards. Although the book aligns with UK standards, because of the common underpinnings in the IFSW definition it has resonance with social work in other countries and therefore is of benefit to students and practice supervisors.

Professional capabilities framework

First devised in 2012, the PCF provides a comprehensive framework outlining what is expected of students at every stage of their education and training from entry to final qualification and for continuing professional development following qualification. The PCF consists of nine domains and aims to provide a holistic approach to identifying and assessing learning needs and outcomes. In 2018, the PCF was reviewed and in addition to the existing nine domains, three 'Super Domains' were included. These cluster the nine domains into three areas with the overarching titles of:

Purpose: *Why we do what we do as social workers, our values and ethics, and how we approach our work.*

Practice: *What we do – the specific skills, knowledge, interventions and critical analytic abilities we develop to act and do social work.*

Impact: *How we make a difference and how we know we make a difference. Our ability to bring about change through our practice, through our leadership, through understanding our context and through our overall professionalism.*

(BASW, 2018)

Each Super Domain is placed over three of the PCF domains. For example, Purpose is placed over Values and Ethics, Diversity and Equality, and Rights, Justice and Economic Well-being. When you explore these domains further, you can see that they are about how we, as social workers, including social work students:

- conduct ourselves,
- understand that diversity characterises and shapes human experience and [this] is critical to the formation of identity,

- recognise and promote the fundamental principles of human rights, social justice and economic well-being.

(BASW, 2018)

However, the principles of Purpose, Practice and Impact can also be seen as overarching all of the domains. For example, 'Purpose' can be directly related to the domain 'Professionalism' including how we conduct ourselves or 'Skills and Interventions', including how we engage with individuals. Furthermore, all nine domains can be directly related to 'Practice', an example being the integration of 'Rights, Justice and Economic Well-being' which is fundamental to social work practice. Each of the nine domains of the PCF has a main statement and an elaboration. Then at each level within the PCF, detailed capabilities have been developed explaining how social workers should expect to evidence that area in practice. The nine domains should be seen as interdependent. The first four levels relate to social work students. These represent the 'level' of capability a social work student should be demonstrating at different points in their social work training. The PCF domains are as follows:

1. *Professionalism* – Identify and behave as a professional social worker, committed to professional development.
2. *Values and Ethics* – Apply social work ethical principles and values to guide professional practices.
3. *Diversity and Equality* – Recognise diversity and apply anti-discriminatory and anti-oppressive principles in practice.
4. *Rights, Justice and Economic Well-being* – Advance human rights and promote social justice and economic well-being.
5. *Knowledge* – Develop and apply relevant knowledge from social work practice and research, social sciences, law, other professional and relevant fields, and from the experience of people who use services.
6. *Critical Reflection and Analysis* – Apply critical reflection and analysis to inform and provide a rationale for professional decision-making.
7. *Skills and Interventions* – Use judgement, knowledge and authority to intervene with individuals, families and communities to promote independence, provide support, prevent harm and enable progress.
8. *Contexts and Organisations* – Engage with, inform and adapt to changing organisational contexts, and the social and policy environments that shape practice. Operate effectively within and contribute to the development of organisations and services, including multi-agency and inter-professional settings.
9. *Professional Leadership* – Promote the profession and good social work practice. Take responsibility for the professional learning and development of others. Develop personal influence and be part of the collective leadership and impact of the profession.

As you progress through your journey to becoming a social worker you should transition from dependency to independence. You will demonstrate your ability to work more autonomously, while at the same time recognising that social workers do not work in isolation. You will recognise your own limitations and identify opportunities for professional development. For example, drawing on the experience and knowledge of other social workers, supervisors and other individuals. Upon completing qualifying programmes, newly qualified social workers should have demonstrated the knowledge, skills and values to work with a range of user groups, the ability to undertake a range of tasks at a foundational level and have the capacity to work with more complex situations.

What's in this book?

Before introducing you to what is covered in each chapter, I would like to talk about the general approach of this book. It is part of a series that outlines and explores the knowledge and skills required for social work practice. It is an example of applied theory and knowledge, with a strong emphasis on how knowledge underpins good social work practice, in addition to developing the skills required. It is written with the future needs of social work students in mind. An action-orientated approach is used to help you develop the knowledge and skills required to work with children and families; with a focus on critical reflection, critical thinking and critical analysis. The emphasis in this book concerns you achieving the requirements of the curriculum, integrating the learning from practice experience gained during placements and developing knowledge and skills that will assist you in meeting the PCF for social work.

In *Chapter 1* you will be introduced to the concepts of profession, professional and professionalism within the context of social work. You will explore what professionalism means, how you 'become' professional and how you practice professionally. We will focus specifically on the PCF domains: Professionalism; Context and Organisations and Professional Leadership, along with the Super Domains: Purpose, Practice, Impact. Additionally, you will also consider the Knowledge and Skills Statement for the Child and Family Practitioner and the UK's four Social Work Professional Body's Professional Standards. Within the chapter there will be an emphasis on preparing for social work practice including communication skills, recognising that social work is multi-disciplinary and the importance of gaining knowledge and understanding of different subject areas. The final section of this chapter will introduce you to critical reflection and the importance of becoming a reflexive social worker. The chapter draws to a close by adding to the discussion relating to preparing for professional practice.

In *Chapter 2* you will explore what is meant by social work values and ethics. You will begin to explore where we get our values from and how values might influence our relationships with other people. You will also consider whether your values inform the decisions that you make. Following our exploration of values, you will explore what is meant by ethics. Building on your understanding of values and ethics, you will look at the ladder of inference. This will be used as a tool to explore our beliefs, how assumptions can be made and how actions can be based on those beliefs and assumptions. The chapter will then introduce a research summary for you to consider values, ethics, beliefs and assumptions in addition to the potential impact of labelling individuals. The research summary and further examples will introduce you to some of the issues associated with labelling and stereotyping. The focus will then switch to exploring cultural awareness and cultural competence, here the notion of cultural humility will be introduced. The emphasis will then turn towards values and ethics and the implications for social work practice where you will return to the discussion relating to preparing for professional practice. The chapter will draw to a close by exploring communicative ethics, narrative ethics, and values and ethics in the digital world.

Chapter 3 will outline Bronfenbrenner's ecological framework and Bourdieu's concepts of habitus, capital and field. You will explore these in relation to social work practice with the focus on working with children and families. You will develop your knowledge gained in Chapter 1 relating to becoming a critically reflexive social worker in relation to Bronfenbrenner's and Bourdieu's theoretical constructs. The chapter will draw to a close by exploring the application of such theories to practice.

In *Chapter 4* the focus will be on family. You will explore the 'traditional' family along with contemporary families. You will be invited to consider your perspectives of what 'family' means and from where these perspectives might originate. You will explore how families are represented within policies. Here you will build on your knowledge gained in Chapter 1 relating to communication and in particular language, and Chapter 2, relating to labelling, and examine how different representations might be oppressive rather than supportive. You will then explore the crucial issue of invisibility and how some families become invisible, but visible by the nature of the label that is attached to them. A research summary will develop your learning further through the examination of family diversity. The chapter will draw to a close by exploring how we describe families and how we display ourselves as a family.

Chapter 5 will focus on exploring how you work with children and young people. Chapter 4 refers to the 'traditional' family and the socialisation of children. In this chapter you will explore how childhood has change, but how the importance of socialisation remains. Reference will be made to the coronavirus pandemic (COVID-19) 2020–2021, and you will consider the potential impact on children. Through a series of scenarios, you will think about how you might prepare to work with children and young people.

Chapter 6 will explore what is meant by safeguarding. This will include exploring what is meant by harm, risk and abuse. Reference will be made to the Children Act 1989 and the Working Together to Safeguard Children: A Guide to Inter-Agency Working to Safeguard and Promote the Welfare of Children 2018 (HM Government, 2020). The latter provides important guidance in relation to safeguarding children and multi-agency working. You will focus on developing your understanding of abuse through the exploration of the four categories identified within the guidance. Through a case study you will explore whether the situation is a safeguarding issue. You will examine the initial reason for social work involvement, but more importantly gain an understanding of the significance of your observations and questioning. An activity will ask whether another situation is a safeguarding issue. Both the case study and activity will enable you to consider safeguarding from different perspectives.

Chapter 7 focuses on the assessment process. You will consider the PCF Super Domains and the importance of having a thorough understanding of the purpose of your involvement. You will then consider aspects of your practice and finally the impact this has made. You will explore the components of the assessment process, developing your understanding of multi-agency working and information sharing. You will develop your skills for gathering information building on the knowledge gained in other chapters and exploring communication and observations. You will look at analysing information and how this important aspect informs your decision-making. You will explore the Framework for the Assessment of Children in Need and their Families and make links to the theories of Bronfenbrenner and Bourdieu discussed previously. Some assessment tools that assist in the gathering of information will be explored.

A Conclusion will summarise the chapters and will invite you to review your learning through revisiting activities and reconsidering your answers. Key themes will be identified.

Learning features

This book is interactive. You are encouraged to work through the book as an active participant, taking responsibility for your learning, in order to increase your knowledge, understanding and ability to apply this learning to practice. Here we can make links with PCF Professional Leadership and taking responsibility for your learning. Each chapter will begin with reference to the relevant aspects of the PCF together with an intro-duction of the chapter contents. Case studies, research summaries and activities throughout the book will help you to reflect on working with children and families. The activities have been created that enable you to reflect on experiences, situations and events and will help you review and summarise the learning undertaken. In this way the knowledge gained will become embedded as part of your professional development. When you come to practise learning in an agency, whether on placement or as a qualified social worker, the work and reflection undertaken here will help you develop your skills and knowledge. In this way, your knowledge will become deeply embedded as part of your development. This book places great emphasis on developing skills in critical reflection including reflecting on practice and preparing for practice.

This book will assist you in developing a questioning approach that looks in a critical way at your thoughts, experiences and practice, as well as key theories and models relating to social work practice. As a result of these deliberations, the book seeks to heighten your skills in taking a critical approach and reflecting on your work within the context of contemporary professional practice. Reflection is central to good social work practice, but only if action and further development result from these reflections. The PCF expects integration of critical reflection across all its domains, and the ability to apply critical reflective skills is a key aspect of social work practice and development. Reflective practice is seen as a key activity to support you with your continuing professional development, therefore maintaining your registration with Social Work England, Northern Ireland Social Care Council, Scottish Social Services Council, Social Care Wales.

Children and young people – definitions of a child

In the UK a child is defined as anyone who has not yet reached their 18th birthday. Therefore, throughout the book the term child/children will be used, rather than using the phrase 'children and young people', unless young people are identified within a specific context.

1

Professionalism

(Continued)

5.15 Communication skills
5.17 Skills in personal and professional development

See Appendix 2 for a detailed description of these standards.

Introduction

In this first chapter we will begin to, in relation to social work, explore the meaning of profession, professional and professionalism. Such exploration is essential because as you set out on your journey undertaking the social work degree, and to becoming a social worker, it is important that you gain an understanding of what is expected of you. However, what does professionalism mean? How do we 'become' professional? How do we practice professionally? These questions will be explored through activities along with exploring the Professional Capabilities Framework (PCF). Reference will also be made to the United Kingdom's (UK) four social work professional bodies: Social Work England (SWE) – Professional Standards (Social Work England, 2020); Wales – Practice Guidance (Social Care Wales, 2017); Scottish Social Service Council – Codes of Practice for Social Service Workers and Employers (Scottish Social Services Council (SSSC), 2016); and Northern Ireland – Standards of Conduct and Practice for Social Workers (Northern Ireland Social Care Council, 2019). Through this journey you will discover how social work involves working collaboratively with a wide range of individuals, and therefore, importance is placed on communication. You will look at different types of communication and the significance of how you conduct, and present, yourself. Social interactions and relationships form the basis of social work practice and therefore communication will be examined within this chapter along with subsequent chapters and throughout the book.

Social workers need to have a wide range of knowledge of different theories, models and perspectives along with an understanding of how these can be applied in practice. You will look at what we mean by knowledge and how knowledge can be gained in many different ways including from working with individuals with lived experiences. Three domains of the PCF – Professionalism, Context and Organisations, and Professional Leadership – will be explored with an emphasis on what represents good social work practice. This will be followed be examining what is meant by reflective and reflexive practice. Firstly, you will be introduced to the dramaturgical approach to reflection and, secondly, reflexivity will be explored through looking at how your own behaviour, mannerisms and assumptions impact on the individuals you are working with. The concepts introduced in this chapter will be developed in further chapters and therefore it is intended that here we lay the foundations of what good social work practice is.

Conduct and presentation

Earlier, we have made reference to how social workers conduct, and present, themselves. These are two different aspects: within a social work context, 'conduct' refers to professional behaviour and the expectation to meet certain standards, for example, the social work professional standards. Whereas, how we 'present' ourselves refers to our presentation of self, including how we dress, how we engage and how we interact with individuals. Here we can see how conduct and presentation of self overlap, for example, communication and language. We could present as being polite and courteous; however, our language could be offensive. This would relate to our conduct and therefore failing to adhere to the professional standards. Throughout the book, we will refer to how we present ourselves, which will include both conduct and presentation of self.

The professionalisation of social work

The professionalisation of social work has a long history; for example, Flexner (1915) concluded that social workers were not professionals, but rather mediators. Social workers did possess the expertism, but referred individuals to professionals such as doctors for medical reasons and teachers for education. Within current social work practice, this is referred to as networking, working in partnership and working collaboratively. Drawing on other professional's expertism provides a more thorough, and evidenced-based, assessment; this will be discussed in Chapter 7. The historical context can also be explored through books such as Timms and Timms (1977). Timms and Timms include three thought-provoking chapters that ask: does social work work?, what should a social worker be able to do?, and what should a social worker know? These are three important questions that are as relevant today as when the book was first written. These will be explored within this chapter and throughout the book. We will return to these three questions as we draw the book to a close. Another interesting book that provides a historical, and also political, context is Jordan (1984). Here Jordan invites us to the 'academic discipline' of social work noting that it is not the same as many other academic disciplines but rather a

> practical activity, in which the personal qualities of the worker may be as important as the knowledge he or she possesses; in which how the worker acts and communicates may be as significant as what he or she decides to do; and the success or failure of which can be evaluated from several different perspectives.

(Jordan, 1984, p. 1)

Activity 1.1

Thinking about the term 'personal qualities', how would you describe personal qualities? Write down four examples of what you understand by personal qualities in relation to your daily life.
Ask yourself why these personal qualities are important in your relationships with other people? For example, family, friends, work colleagues.

Comment

You may have identified the importance of how you present yourself and how you communicate with others, such as do you present yourself as being confident, knowledgeable and approachable, do you listen to what people say, do you consider their different perspectives, and do you consider the words you use when in conversation with other people? These qualities and characteristics will be explored further within this chapter and throughout the book.

For a more recent and comprehensive examination into the history of social work, including global social work, see Parker and Finch (2020), and for professional social work and social work identity, see Parker and Doel (2013). The former examines the early beginnings of social work, the poor law and the subsequent amendment, the emergence of social problems and social reforms, whereas the latter explores some of the contested meanings and developments of social work along with the history and sociological context of professionalism and professions.

Exploring the meaning of profession, professional and professionalism

The terms profession, professional and professionalism are open to interpretation. They are frequently used to describe job roles, how individuals undertake those roles or how an individual presents themselves. However, as Parker and Doel (2013) suggest, if you can act professionally, you can also act unprofessionally. Therefore, consideration needs to be given to differentiate between professional and unprofessional. Here we are guided by the PCF (British Association of Social Workers (BASW), 2018) and the UK's four social work professional bodies: SWE – Professional Standards; Wales – Practice Guidance; SSSC – Codes of Practice for Social Service Workers and Employers; and Northern Ireland – Standards of Conduct and Practice for Social Workers (see Table 1.1). When we consider the three terms, profession, professional and professionalism, they also relate to expertise, being qualified and belonging to a professional body. However, we also need to consider how an individual may represent their profession, for example, social work. Phrases such as 'the social worker demonstrated good social work values' are frequently heard, but also consider how social workers are often represented in the media.

Activity 1.2

Thinking about the people you know and your experiences of interacting with different people, what do the terms profession, professional and professionalism mean to you? Write three sentences for each of the following:

Profession
Professional
Professionalism

Comment

Thinking about the above exercise, did you consider any specific qualities such as individual characteristics, mannerisms, behaviours, skills, job roles, qualifications or other aspects that denote a profession, being a professional or when we would use the term professionalism? What was important to you about these terms?

Activity 1.3

Following Activity 1.2, join your sentences together to form a paragraph. When writing your paragraph, consider what makes a social worker a professional, how does a social worker practice professionally and conclude your paragraph with a sentence outlining your reflections on these two final points.

Comment

In Activity 1.3, you re-visited the sentences you wrote in Activity 1.2 to create a paragraph. Here, you considered what makes a social worker a professional and how a social worker practices professionally. You concluded your paragraph with a sentence outlining your reflections on these two final points. Take one more look at your paragraph, would you add anything further? Could you now write three bullet points identifying what you intend to do, at university and during your placements, to demonstrate how you could present yourself professionally. For example, in order to develop my knowledge and understanding of professional practice I will become more aware of my actions, interactions and the manner in which I present myself. Now explain how you could become more aware. What would you need to do; how would you know when you have done it? Have you included any timescales? For example, in three months I will return to, and complete again, Activities 1.2 and 1.3 and compare my two paragraphs.

What does being a social worker mean to me

As you progress through the social work degree, such terms will become much clearer as your knowledge increases and you have a greater understanding of the social work role. As I write this book, I reflect on what these terms mean to me as a social worker. As a social worker I belong to a profession. The profession has a professional body and therefore I need to be appropriately qualified in order to register with it. To call myself a social worker, which is a protected title, I need to be qualified. As a social worker, I am observed as a professional, I represent the social work profession and therefore there is a requirement to uphold the professional body's professional standards. To uphold these standards I have responsibilities, I need to be accountable, I need to be aware of my actions and interactions (see Table 1.1). This also includes my personal life and what is often overlooked by many people is that this includes how I use social media and thus I need to be digitally responsible (Taylor, 2017).

Professional standards

Through the Professional Standards (SWE); Practice Guidance (Wales); Codes of Practice for Social Service Workers and Employers (SSSC); and the Standards of Conduct and Practice for Social Workers (Northern Ireland), as outlined in Table 1.1, we are able to identify the importance of developing self-care skills, developing and maintaining relationships, working collaboratively, maintaining trust, developing confidence, safeguarding, promoting good practice including promoting the rights and interests of individuals, in addition to taking responsibility for our own learning and development. As you progress, you will develop your knowledge and understanding of social work practice along with the many different theories, models, perspectives and the legislative framework. You will also integrate your learning with practice experience gained through placements and thus your social work identity will begin to develop. As your journey through the social work degree course approaches the end, your identity, that of a newly qualified social worker (NQSW), will emerge as you enter the Assessed and Supported Year in Employment (ASYE), see Table 1.1.

Professional practice

Along with personal qualities and practicing in a professional manner, you also need to have knowledge. Shulman explains that

> professional education is not education for understanding alone; it is preparation for accomplished and responsible practice in the service of others. It is preparation for 'good work'. Professionals must learn abundant amounts of theory and vast bodies of knowledge. They must come to understand in order to act, and they must act in order to serve.

(Shulman, 2005, p. 53)

As you start out on your journey, it may feel quite daunting when you think about all that you need to know. It is important to remember that knowledge can be gained in many different ways including experience. We have now started to identify that a social worker needs both personal qualities, which facilitate acting professionally, and knowledge, in order to undertake the role of a social worker. We have introduced the terms profession, professional and professionalism. Such terms may exemplify characteristics, qualifications, knowledge and experience. Shulman (2005) suggests that professional education is preparation for responsible practice. Responsible practice includes presentation of self and commitment to studying and self-development. We will add to this as we progress through the chapters. Figure 1.1 places preparation for professional practice into context.

Table 1.1 UK social work professional standards; practice guidance; codes of practice for social service workers and employers; standards of conduct and practice for social workers

Social work England – Professional standards	Wales – Practice guidance	Scottish social service council – Codes of practice for social service workers and employers	Northern Ireland – Standards of conduct and practice for social workers
Promote the rights, strengths and well-being of people, families and communities.	Person-centred social work.	As a social service worker, I must protect and promote the rights and interests of people who use services and carers.	As a social worker, you must protect the rights and promote the interests and well-being of service users and carers.
Establish and maintain the trust and confidence of people.	Good social work practice.	As a social service worker, I must create and maintain the trust and confidence of people who use services and carers.	As a social worker, you must strive to establish and maintain the trust and confidence of service users and carers.
Be accountable for the quality of my practice and the decisions I make.	Safeguarding individuals.	As a social service worker, I must promote the independence of people who use services while protecting them, as far as possible, from danger and harm.	As a social worker, you must promote the autonomy of service users while safeguarding them as far as possible from danger or harm.
Maintain my continuing professional development.	Developing and managing self.	As a social service worker, I must respect the rights of people who use services, while striving to make sure that their behaviour does not harm themselves or other people.	As a social worker, you must respect the rights of service users while seeking to ensure that their behaviour does not harm themselves or other people.
Act safely, respectfully and with professional integrity.	Working with colleagues.	As a social service worker, I must uphold public trust and confidence in social services.	As a social worker, you must uphold public trust and confidence in social care services. As a social worker, you must be accountable for the quality of your work and take responsibility for maintaining and improving your knowledge and skills.
Promote ethical practice and report concerns.	Contributing to service improvement.	As a social service worker, I am accountable for the quality of my work and will take responsibility for maintaining and improving my knowledge and skills.	As a social worker, you must protect the rights and promote the interests and well-being of service users and carers.
	Good conduct.		

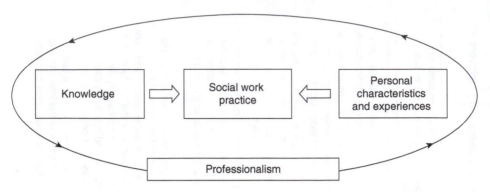

Figure 1.1 Preparation for professional practice

Professional capabilities framework

Following an exploration of profession, professional and professionalism, let's introduce the PCF (British Association of Social Workers (BASW), 2018). The PCF is a framework for nine levels of social work in England (see Appendix 1). There are four pre-qualifying levels: Point of Entry, Readiness for Practice, End of First Placement and End of Last Placement. The remaining five levels are all qualifying levels. There are nine domains and three super domains. Each super domain is placed above three domains; however, they also relate to the other domains and therefore all of the domains are interwoven. All of the domains directly relate to social work practice. The PCF domains are illustrated as a fan; see Appendix 1. As we work through the chapters, we will continue to make reference to the PCF domains and how they relate to practice. We will not refer to the full domain level descriptors; these can be accessed on the BASW website. Additionally, BASW also includes the 'Digital Capabilities Statement for Social Work', which is a 'framework to guide practice. It identifies the knowledge, skills and values social workers need to develop their use of digital technology in practice' (BASW).

Activity 1.4

Go to the BASW website and look at the PCF level descriptor for Professionalism. Can you identify the similarities and differences between the different levels (Point of Entry, Readiness for Practice, End of First Placement and End of Last Placement/Completion)?

Comment

On closer inspection of the PCF domain Professionalism, firstly, we can see that we need to 'identify and behave as a professional social worker, committed to professional development'. In Activity 1.1 you identified the various characteristics relating to profession, professional and professionalism. Within this domain you can see the need to identify and behave professionally, in addition to being committed to continuing professional learning and development. As we work across the columns of the domain, we can see the four levels and the level descriptors below each level. At entry level you are expected to be able to demonstrate an initial understanding of social work and have commitment to becoming a social worker, in addition to recognising your own strengths, initial understanding of the importance of self-care and to take responsibility for your own learning. With each level, the expectations and responsibilities increase; however, your knowledge and understanding should also increase through your academic studies, practice experience gained through placements and reflecting on your studies and practice, thus integrating your learning.

Activity 1.5

Return to Activity 1.3, and the paragraph you wrote, now take a look at the PCF domain Professionalism and see if you can identify any characteristics, phrases or commonalities between your observations and the similarities and differences you noted in Activity 1.4.
Return to your paragraph, is there anything you would add or remove, if so, why?

Comment

Through these activities you are beginning to identify the characteristics of a professional social worker including how you should present, communicate and be committed to continuing professional development. Following Activity 1.5, it is observed that these attributes are a requirement and as such a social worker needs to demonstrate professional integrity and accountability at all times.

The importance of communication

Relationships

Professionalism, and particularly how a social worker presents themselves in terms of their presentation, demeanour, reliability, honesty and respectfulness along with communicating with others, is essential in building and maintaining relationships. Wonnacott (2012) describes social work as involving 'the capacity to develop and maintain relationships, manage the emotional dimension of the work and make judgements and decisions, often in the light of conflicting information' (p. 13). Trevithick (2012) observes that relationship building is based 'on the knowledge, skills, values and qualities, which social workers bring to the work' (p. 164). We are able to identify aspects of both of these quotations within the PCF domains. When we think about how a social worker presents themselves, consideration should be given to communication, which is essential in not only building relationships but also ending relationships. Ending relationships appropriately is a must. When working with children and their parents you need to discuss timescales, how long will you be working with them, and endings. Your assessment and intervention will be time limited. This is important when working with children who could become attached and distressed when suddenly they realise that you are no longer involved. Parents also need to be informed. Therefore, it is vitally important to discuss the piece of work to be undertaken with clarity, openness and honesty. Additionally, you do not want to create an attachment and/or dependency, but rather independence. Here we see the importance of communication skills. Communication could be described as either verbal or non-verbal; see Figure 1.2.

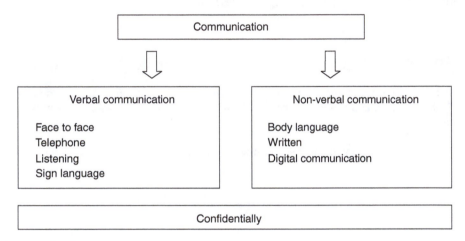

Figure 1.2   Communication

Communication skills

Communication and interpersonal skills are significant within social work. A social worker needs to articulate clearly and succinctly what they have to say using words that are understood by all the individuals they are working with (Koprowska, 2020). Whether meeting someone for the first time, or when you have built a relationship with an individual, you need to be mindful of verbal and non-verbal communication, listen attentively and clarify your understanding of what they have said, what has been discussed and agreed. The words you use, how you say something and the manner in which you say it, along with your body language all play a part in effective communication. You will develop these skills through academic engagement and during your placements.

Acronyms

When we are communicating, the use of acronyms can be confusing, misleading and misinterpreted. Many individuals will not be familiar with a series of letters and thus, what the acronym stands for. Other professionals might have the same acronym, but it means something completely different. Imagine attending a multi-agency meeting and the following acronyms are being used, what do they mean?

- CAMHS
- CSE
- MARAC
- PIES
- SCR

A list of acronyms can be found at the beginning of the book.

Euphemisms

Another confusing and misleading aspect of communication is euphemisms. Fearnley (2012) observes that 'the language adopted when communicating with children about their parent's illness strongly influences how they begin to make sense of what is happening or conversely how they make mis-meaning from the situation' (p. 42). This quotation is about working with children in a very specific situation, but it illustrates the importance of the language we use. Therefore, it is essential that communication, verbal and non-verbal including written or digital forms, is clearly, sensitively and effectively articulated. We can see that without effective communication there is the possibility of misunderstanding or misinterpretation and actions or interactions might not be appropriately implemented. Consequently, children may be placed at risk of significant harm. Significant harm will be explored in Chapter 6.

Confidentiality

With regards to communication and being professional, another important factor to consider is that of confidentiality. This includes sharing information (see the Data Protection Act 2018 and General Data Protection Regulation (GDPR)), and therefore it is important to be aware of where we are, who we are with and who can hear what is being talked about. The Working Together to Safeguard Children: A Guide to Inter-Agency Working to Safeguard and Promote the Welfare of Children 2018 (HM Government, 2020), discussed in Chapter 6, provides a comprehensive guide to sharing information. Sharing of information includes verbally, written and through digital formats.

> **Case study**
>
> You are on a train, the carriage is full, and a male makes a telephone call. His voice is loud and although you are a few seats away you can hear every word. You are reading a book, but are distracted by the telephone call. The male refers to himself as Doctor Forrest, and states which hospital he is a based at. He begins talking about a patient and
>
> *(Continued)*

(Continued)

although the details are sparse, you think to yourself I do not need to know about the patient, and you continue to read. The doctor then makes a second telephone call and discusses another patient. He refers to the patient's name, you stop reading your book, the patient's diagnosis is discussed and this time the information is in much more detail.
What are your immediate thoughts?
How would you feel if it was one of your family members or a friend he was talking about?

Comment

The doctor is sharing information inappropriately, breaching confidentiality and acting unprofessionally. If this information was about a family member you might contact them to express your feelings about their diagnosis. What if they had not yet been informed of the diagnosis? What if they were aware of the diagnosis, but had decided not to inform family members? This provides an example of the importance of being self-aware when discussing service user's information and that it should not occur in any public space or place. Another location to think about is the communal area of lifts in public buildings. Imagine the following scenario – two colleagues returning to the office following a meeting discuss the outcomes in the lift. Who else is in the lift? Do they need to know? Be conscious, self-aware and remember the Data Protection Act (2018) only share information that is appropriate and where confidentiality is assured.

Communication in practice

Communication is essential when working with individuals, building networks and working in organisations. Communication, relationship building and networking are all important skills. Additionally, we need to consider self-management, for example, being aware of, and regulating our emotions, considering our value base, assumptions and beliefs. These are all areas identified within the PCF domain Context and Organisations. This domain refers to engaging, informing and adapting to changing organisational contexts. There is also reference here to how policy and social environments shape practice along with the need to work effectively, contribute to the development of organisations and services. Here you see the significance of multi-agency and inter-professional working, this will be explored further in Chapter 6. We can also begin to see the relationship between the two domains Professionalism and Context and Organisations.

Presentation of self

Presentation of self is evident within both the Professionalism and Context and Organisations domains. If communication is crucial in relationship building, it also needs to be acknowledged that sometimes social workers need to challenge other individuals. This needs a calm, sensitive approach; attentively listening to their perspectives while at the same time providing a clear rationale for their involvement, their intervention and what will happen next. This is a skill that will develop with experience. A suggestion for developing your skills would be to observe how social workers and other professionals challenge. This might include listening to what questions they ask to gather information, raise concerns and how they apply, and articulate, policies and procedures in practice. You need to develop a professional curiosity, a critical questioning approach, asking the why, what, when and how questions to gain knowledge and understanding. Additionally, social workers have a role in shaping and challenging organisational structures. This will be discussed in Chapter 2.

Professional leadership

The PCF domain Professional Leadership includes promoting the profession and good social work practice, along with taking responsibility for your learning and development. Also included in this domain is sharing, supporting and working collaboratively to assist others in their learning and development. Social work is a multi-disciplinary profession and therefore, as we talked about earlier, a social worker needs a wide range of knowledge, but also the ability to apply that knowledge in practice and share with others. The PCF domain Knowledge states:

Develop and apply relevant knowledge from social work practice and research, social sciences, law, other professional and relevant fields, and from the experience of people who use services.

Exploring knowledge in the context of social work

Social work is multi-disciplinary

It can be seen that social workers develop knowledge through many different sources including through experiences and from individuals with lived experiences. It is important that we recognise and acknowledge that we can learn from these individuals when we listen to their experiences, stories and their journey to where they are today, and take time to talk to them. As you progress through your journey to becoming a social worker, you will begin to understand that social work is a multi-disciplinary profession and as such draws on many different disciplines; some of these are identified in Table 1.2.

Table 1.2 Social work draws on many different disciplines

Anthropology	Philosophy
Economics	Politics
Law	Psychology
Leadership and management	Social Policy
Neuroscience (a subdivision of biology)	Sociology

This is not an exhaustive list, but does begin to show the broad range of disciplines that informs social work practice, many of which have subfields. For example, cultural anthropology, social anthropology, community psychology, social psychology and cognitive psychology are all relevant to social work. As you begin your social work journey, it would be useful to explore these along with identifying others. For example, social anthropology examines how people live in the contemporary world, social psychology studies the behaviour of individuals in their social and cultural settings, and the various fields of philosophy explore ethics, morals and logic – the reasoning informing our arguments. These three areas alone provide a wealth of knowledge and understanding of how people live. They provide insights into behaviour, ethics, morals and reasons for the way they live as they do, in addition to providing an explanation to why they might behave in certain ways. When exploring different theories, models and perspectives always think critically about their strengths, limitations and unpinning philosophy 'a sceptical, analytic or questioning approach taken to the theories and models rather than simple acceptance' (Parker, 2020, p. 86).

Accumulating knowledge

As you read this, you may be asking where do we accumulate such knowledge from. Knowledge can be gained through different ways including academic studies, reading, reflection, experience and through talking to, and working with, different individuals. Knowledge can be defined as being explicit or tacit (Trevithick, 2012, Teater, 2020).

Table 1.3 Knowledge – explicit and tacit

Explicit knowledge	Tacit knowledge
Theories	'Gut' feelings
Models	Emotions
Approaches	Insights
Perspectives	Intuition
Policies and proceedings	Observations
Legislation	Experiences

Again, this is not an exhaustive list; however, what we can observe is that explicit knowledge underpins a social worker's practice, for example, child development theory, task-centred model, systemic practice approach and strengths perspective.

Tacit knowledge has the potential to influence a social worker's practice; however, a significant difference is that explicit knowledge is usually, but not always, based on fact, evidence or theory. A process has been undertaken to ascertain the facts. With tacit knowledge we need to think about how a 'gut' feeling or an emotion can be evidenced. Therefore, we can begin to see the importance of integrating theory to practice. Nevertheless, both explicit and tacit knowledge may contribute towards meaning-making, making sense of different circumstances and situations and making decisions. We also need to acknowledge that a social worker would not go to court and report a 'feeling'; for example, 'I felt that the child was at risk', factual evidence would be required. A social worker may feel that a child is at risk, but it is through the assessment process, discussed in Chapter 7, that they gather the evidence to demonstrate how the child is at risk. The social worker would need to be aware of confirmation bias. In other words, the evidence needs to be factual and not biased towards proving the child was at risk to illustrate the initial feelings were correct. We will explore these areas further as we progress through the chapters.

What should a social worker know?

We will now return to the question posed at the beginning of this chapter: what knowledge should a social worker know? The Knowledge and Skills Statement for Child and Family Practitioners (Department for Education, 2018) identifies ten areas of what a social worker should know:

1. Relationships and effective direct work
2. Communication
3. Child development
4. Adult mental health, substance misuse, domestic abuse, physical ill health and disability
5. Abuse and neglect of children
6. Child and family assessment
7. Analysis, decision-making, planning and review
8. The law and the family and youth justice systems
9. The role of supervision
10. Organisational context

We have touched on many of these areas already and as we progress through the book we will return to and make links to others. We will also make connections between the Knowledge and Skills Statement, PCF and Professional Standards. As Shulman (2005) noted, 'professionals must learn abundant amounts of theory and vast bodies of knowledge' (p. 53), but how do we learn such amounts of knowledge?

Walker et al. (2008), although writing about practice education, provide an excellent resource for social work students. Chapter 2, *What Is Learning*, includes the continuous spiral of professional development and learning. The continuous spiral takes you on a learning journey, developing confidence, new knowledge, increasing understanding, embedding this knowledge in practice, exploring new ideas, generating and engaging in debate and identifying areas for further development.

Professional development

Applying such an approach to your learning will enable you to gain a greater understanding of different theories, models and perspectives. Through a process of reading, critical reflection and debate, learning will be consolidated. Additionally, through making links between modules studied at university, and practice experience gained during placements, practice becomes underpinned by theory and embedded within a legislative framework. It is important to remember that social work also has a human dimension and thus it is inevitably that building, maintaining and ending relationships will also be determined by your own presentation of self. Therefore, there is an element of learning about oneself, questioning your own values, feelings and emotions and how these might influence your own practice. This relates to the PCF; 'recognise the impact my own values and attitudes can have on relationships with others' (PCF domain Values and Ethics). This will be explored further in Chapter 2. Additionally, we need to have an understanding of the wider issues, such as social, economic and political, which affect organisations, communities and individuals including children, young people and families.

Professional leadership

What we have been exploring lies within the PCF domain Professional Leadership. Within this domain we can see that importance is placed on the promotion of good social work practice; 'we develop and show our leadership, individually and collectively, through promoting social work's purpose, practices and impact' (BASW, 2018). When we talk about professional development, we are referring to continuing professional growth, learning and development. Earlier in the chapter we referred to the social work degree as a journey and it is this journey that will enable you to learn about yourself, work collaboratively and develop professionally.

Reflective and reflexive practice

Reflection

Critical reflection is a significant part of the journey of professional development and social work practice. Through the process of reflection, you will be able to think about what you have done and why. This might include thinking about a conversation, an event, activity or intervention. Some of your reflections might include asking yourself whether you did it in such a way because you were taught to do it that way, because you have always done it that way or because you do not know any other way of doing it. When thinking about these questions, you may see that how you approached a situation might have been the best way, the only way; however, on reflection, there might be other ways of doing it. Critically reflecting on what you did, why, how and what was underpinning your work will enable you to evaluate and learn from the experience. The process of reflection is shown in Figure 1.3.

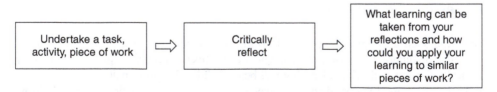

Figure 1.3 Process of critical reflection

Reflection may be undertaken alone such as writing a reflective account or with others during discussions, tutorials and supervision sessions. However, and importantly, it is the learning taken from those reflections that is significant. This is why it is very important to record those reflections and by doing so you are able to record the learning taken from the situation, along with the subsequent action plan of how you are going to implement the learning and again the reflections on the learning and action plan. Many people find that a learning journal is an excellent resource to record their reflections, actions and development. Here we can begin to see a cycle of reflection. There are many different models of reflection including Kolb (1984), Gibbs (1988) and Schön (1983) (see Mantell and Scragg, 2019). When qualified you will need to demonstrate continuing professional development through critical reflection for SWE and re-registration.

Dramaturgical approach to reflection

I would like to introduce you to the dramaturgical approach to reflection. This approach of reflection is a fluid model, which encourages deeper reflection in many different dimensions. The dramaturgical model of social interaction is most associated with Goffman. Goffman's seminal text *The Presentation of Self in Everyday Life* (1959/1990) applies a theatrical language to everyday life and refers to individuals as actors who perform. Goffman uses the terms scripts, scenes, front stage and back stage, all of which you will recognise as being the language of the theatre. The 'dramaturgic' relates to self, to social interactions and how we as individuals perform to the wider world – the front stage (to an audience) or the back stage (when we are not performing to an audience). Goffman observes how individuals perform.

> *The perspective employed in this report is that of the theatre performance; the principles derived are dramaturgical ones. I shall consider the way in which the individual in ordinary work situations presents himself and his activity to others, the ways in which he guides and controls the impression they form of him, and the kinds of things he may not do while sustaining his performance before them.*

> (Goffman, 1959, p. xi).

> *It is probably no mere historical accident that the word person, in its first meaning, is a mask. It is rather a recognition of the fact that everyone is always and everywhere, more or less consciously, playing a role ... It is in these roles that we know each other; it is in these roles that we know ourselves.*

> (Park, R. E. 1950, Race and Culture, Illinois: The Free Press, p. 249 –
> cited in Goffman, 1990)

> *In a sense, and in so far as this mask represents the conception we have formed of ourselves – the role we are striving to live up to – this mask is our truer self, the self we would like to be. In the end, our conception of our role becomes second nature and an*

integral part of our personality. We come into the world as individuals, achieve character, and become persons.

(Park, R. E. 1950, Race and Culture, Illinois: The Free Press, p. 249 –
cited in Goffman, 1990).

These three quotations epitomise the suggestion that we are all performers. Every day we are performing to a wide range of audiences, at home, with friends and at work.

Activity 1.6

Think for a moment how you perform with those individuals you feel comfortable with? Does your performance change if another individual joins you – maybe someone you know or maybe someone you don't know? For example, think about the following scenario:

You have arranged to meet a group of friends in a local café. The group is well established and you all get on well. While talking, another friend joins the group, however, they have brought along one of their friends, someone who you have not met before.

How do you behave with the new person in the group? How do you react? What are your thoughts, feelings, does your performance change?

Comment

Think about the social worker and their performance with a wide range of audiences. The social worker presents themselves to a family, the parents, the children, to colleagues, managers and other professionals. They work in partnership to undertake and complete assessments. The social worker might have to present their findings at court. For each performance:

- the script will have variations;
- the language used may differ as the characters change, for example, the parents, children, professionals or when addressing a judge;
- each individual playing a different role;
- venues may change; and
- in each environment, there is the potential for the audience to change.

The dramaturgical model is illustrated through a series of scenarios. We will explore each of these in relation to the social work role. This is illustrated in Figure 1.4.

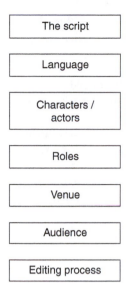

Figure 1.4 Dramaturgical model

The script – placing the event, situation, circumstance into context. The telephone call, the home visit, the direct work with the child. The script sets the scene; this may be a referral, additional information or a report. It could also be the assessment.

The language – the social worker needs to consider language, avoid jargon, acronyms, colloquialisms and euphemisms and articulate clearly the purpose of their involvement, reasons for actions, recommendations and what will happen next. The social worker may adapt their language for the parents, children, colleagues, managers and other professionals. Language also refers to tone, level and the manner in which the words are spoken. Also consider both verbal and non-verbal communication, written communication and body language.

The characters/actors – who's involved. Within any situation, it is likely that there will be many different characters/actors. For example, the social worker, their manager, other team members, parents, children, grandparents, wider family members, friends, senior managers/directors, other professionals, judges, lawyers, barristers, foster carers, the list is endless. We can see therefore that the social worker performs to a wide range of audiences, and how they perform is dependent on the script. Within each performance they need to take into consideration their language during that performance. There are many different tools available for identifying family composition and support networks, some of these will be explored in Chapter 7. We also need to note that each individual will be performing and therefore, as Goffman (1959/1990) suggests, the performance will be what that individual wants us to see, the impression they wish to give; the front stage. However, we also need to consider the back stage and what the performers are not saying, doing or maybe hiding from us. These areas will be examined through a case study in Chapter 7.

The roles – within any given situation there are always a number of individuals, each playing their role. For example, each member of the family, parents, children, maybe grandparents, have their role to play within the context of family life, here we can observe a myriad of interconnected relationships, which the social worker needs to be aware of, recognise and acknowledge. The social work role is complex, there are many different roles including undertaking assessments, protecting and safeguarding, supporting and advocating on behalf of children and adults and at times simultaneously. We also need to remember that social workers do not work in isolation, but within an inter-professional and multi-agency approach and as such work in partnership with other professionals too. We will explore these areas in greater detail in Chapter 6. Once again, we can see a myriad of interconnected relationships.

The venue – including the setting, environment, location. The social worker may be undertaking their role in many different settings including the office, the family home, a school, a hospital, a court. Each venue may have its own etiquette. In the family home the social worker needs to respect the family's space while at the same time undertake their work such as completing an assessment. The courtroom will have its own customs. It requires a dress code to be followed, a way of addressing the judge, the barristers and other members of the courtroom. As the venue changes, the expectations may change, the language may change and the social worker might add clarity to the initial script, present their assessment or evidence. Whatever the venue, it is important to remember confidentiality as discussed previously.

The audience – the audience is the individual or individuals who the social worker is working with, or addressing. Each individual, character/actor, plays their role, their performance may vary depending on the audience and on the other characters/actors. The venue may change. The language may differ as the social worker presents themselves to others. The social worker recognises, acknowledges and values the audience whether they are presenting information to an individual or a group of individuals during a meeting. Through experience, the social worker becomes skilled in articulating information clearly and succinctly and is able to present to the audience in a non-judgemental manner, using language that is not patronising, and which is easy to understand. It is always important to remember the professional standards by which we work, and thus the social worker should always be respectful, polite and courteous; and at all times be professional, as they represent the profession and demonstrate professionalism.

The editing process – the social worker will edit their communication, their language, their presentation of self, depending on the message they wish to convey. This will include verbal, non-verbal and/or written. The social worker reports an edited version to their manager of what they observed during a home visit, what the parents reported and what the children reported. They write an edited version of their case notes, chronology, assessment and report. While this editing is undertaken using a different language for the various audiences, the information must remain factual so that consistent information is being presented.

The dramaturgical approach in practice

A key strength of the dramaturgical approach is the emphasis on thinking about the different contexts, roles and environments the social worker might experience within practice. As we make our way through the book, this approach will become much clearer as we refer to the scenarios while considering the different topics in each chapter. This approach to reflection is typically used for reflecting on practice, doing something, for example, following a home visit or the completion of an assessment. The latter, for example, would include breaking down the whole assessment process, considering each of the seven scenarios in relation to your practice and critically reflecting on the what, why, when and how you did every piece of work that contributed to the assessment. This would identify what worked, what did not work as you expected, what you would do differently next time and areas for further development. Within the book we will use this approach of reflection to plan how you might undertake a piece of work, for example, what you might consider prior to the home visit. On placement, for example, you could use this model of reflection to plan a piece of work, such as gathering wishes and feelings when working with a child, and again reflect on the work undertaken. In Chapter 5, we will explore this approach to reflection in more detail.

Reflexivity

Another significant factor to consider when thinking about professionalism is that of reflexivity. Critical reflexivity includes examining the role of emotions and how emotions might influence our practice and decision-making (Ingram, 2013). Reflexivity, according to Cunliffe (2004), 'means examining critically the assumptions underlying our actions, the impact of those actions, and from a broader perspective, what passes as good management practice' (p. 407).

What Cunliffe is describing is relevant to social work. The 'good management practice' of social work includes social work values, anti-oppressive and anti-discriminatory practice along with having an awareness of one's mannerisms, behaviour and presentation of self and the potential impact these aspects may have on others. Therefore, a critically reflexive social worker is one who questions and self-examines their own assumptions, values, beliefs and presentation of self on others. They apply a critical questioning approach evaluating their actions and interactions including verbal and non-verbal communication and their relationships with others. The good management of practice also aligns with the PCF domain Professional Leadership.

The social worker who is critically reflexive 'draws upon very different ways of thinking about the nature of reality' (Cunliffe, 2004, p. 408). The good management of social work practice is therefore how we present, manage our practice and maintain our professional development. This is congruent with the professional standards, PCF and Knowledge and Skills Statement for Child and Family Partitioners. According to D'Cruz et al. (2007), there are three variations of the meaning of reflexivity. The first variation relates to the individual's ability to process information and create knowledge. This relates to the social worker's ability to understand information, knowing what processes to follow and generating knowledge for the purpose of knowing the next course of action. For example, the social worker thoroughly understands the referral, the purpose of their involvement and what they need to do next, and why, and through the assessment process is able to generate new knowledge and understanding in relation to the situation and circumstances in which they are working. The second variation describes reflexivity as an individual's self-critical approach. The individual questions their beliefs and assumptions and explores the world around them from multiple perspectives. They apply a self-examining approach to what they are doing including why and how. They also explore power between relationships including relationships between individuals and between individuals and organisational structures. The third variation examines how emotions influence a social worker's practice.

The reflexive social worker

The reflexive social worker is likely to have a greater understanding of how they present themselves and how their emotions might influence their ability to build, develop and maintain relationships. The critically reflexive social worker is able to explore the moral dimensions of their work ensuring that their practice and subsequent decision-making is ethical and supported by factual evidence. These dimensions are interwoven throughout the professional standards, PCF and Knowledge and Skills Statement for Child and Family Practitioners. How we present ourselves, our behaviours, attitudes, approaches and perspectives might be instinctive, but they can also be learnt. Additionally, we need to ensure confidentiality, consider the information we are sharing and how we are presenting ourselves and how we are using social media and being digitally responsible (Taylor, 2017). As a social worker we need to promote good social work values and demonstrate commitment to challenging, promoting and empowering individuals (see Table 1.3).

The social work degree includes placements. The integration of the academic learning and practice experience is essential in the preparation for professional practice. We also need to be able to critically reflect on our practice and remind ourselves that if we can act professionally, we can also act unprofessionally (Parker and Doel, 2013). Building on Figure 1.1, we can add communication and becoming a reflective and reflexive social worker. We are now beginning to identify the foundations of professional social work practice – see Figure 1.5.

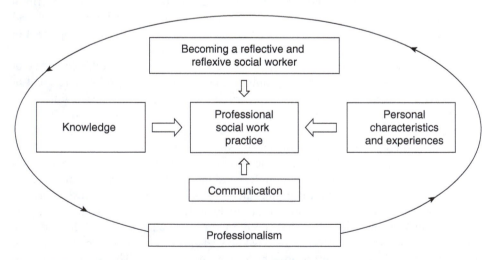

Figure 1.5 Foundations of professional social work practice

Chapter summary

In this chapter, we have introduced and started to explore some of the key features relating to professional, profession and professionalism. We have made links to the professional standards, PCF and Knowledge and Skills Statement for the Child and Family Practitioner. We have started to explore the significance of communication, the importance of knowledge and becoming a reflective and reflexive social worker. The next chapter will explore values and ethics relating to social work and therefore will build on, and develop, some of the concepts identified in this chapter, for example, communication, knowledge and good social work practice.

Further reading

Koprowska, J (2020) *Communication and Interpersonal Skills in Social Work*. London: Sage/ Learning Matters.

This book explores the communication and interpersonal skills needed for social work practice. This includes non-verbal communication, emotional expression and working with children and families. Chapters also explore communication skills in relation to working with individuals with additional needs along with group working, involuntary service users and hostility.

Parker, J (ed.) (2020) *Introducing Social Work*. London: Sage/Learning Matters.

Each of the chapters in this edited book considers social work knowledge, skills and practice. The book explores social work theory and methods, integrates theory and practice and includes specific areas of social work practice. This book provides a comprehensive introduction to social work practice from different perspectives.

Useful websites

BASW: https://www.basw.co.uk/social-work-training/professional-capabilities-framework-pcf.

BASW: https://www.basw.co.uk/resources/publications-policies-and-reports/digital-capabilities-social-workers.

2

Values and ethics

It will also introduce you to the following standards as set out in the Social Work Subject Benchmark Statement (2019):

4.6   Social work is an ethical activity...
5.3   Values and Ethics
5.4   Service Users and Carers
5.14 vi. critically analyse and take account of the impact of inequality and discrimination in working with people who use social work services.
5.16 Skills in working with others
5.17 i.   work at all times in accordance with codes of professional conduct and ethics.
5.17 vii. be open and honest with people if things go wrong

See Appendix 2 for a detailed description of these standards.

Introduction

Following on from the previous chapter, this chapter will examine what is meant by social work values and ethics. The interconnectedness between values and ethics and the notion of becoming a professional will be considered throughout this chapter. We will begin by exploring where we get our values from and how values might influence our relationships with other people. We will also consider whether values inform the decisions we make. Following our exploration of values, we will examine what is meant by ethics. Building on your understanding of values and ethics, you will be introduced to the ladder of inference. This will be used as a tool to explore beliefs and assumptions and how these might influence our actions and interactions. Through a Research Summary you will explore how values, ethics, beliefs and assumptions might result in labelling and stereotyping. This will be followed by an exploration of cultural awareness, cultural competence and cultural humility. We will then turn our attention to focus on social work practice and build on the concepts introduced in Chapter 1. Finally, the chapter will explore communicative ethics, narrative ethics, and values and ethics in the digital world.

What do we mean by values and ethics?

Any chapter examining values and ethics has to begin with the question what are values and what are ethics? Another question you might ask is what have values and ethics to do with social work? Exploring values and ethics can be exciting and challenging, but also daunting and at times may feel overwhelming because of the philosophical foundations. As a social worker, you will need to explore, question and challenge your own value base. You will work with individuals, make decisions in relation to their lives, and many of these decisions are likely to have an impact throughout their lives. For example, when you make a decision in relation to a child, the decision could impact that child's life, not just through childhood but through adulthood as well. Therefore, you will need to ensure that you are applying an ethical decision-making approach. We will return to this later in the chapter. Firstly, let us explore what we mean by values and ethics, which are frequently described and defined in many different ways. The two are often intertwined and thus seen as one; however, there are significant differences. Values relate to an individual's beliefs or principles. These may be personal values, cultural values and community values, which place importance on certain aspects of doing something in a particular manner. Values are not universal and may change over time. Whereas, ethics are underpinned by theoretical constructs and have legal and moral duties.

What are values?

When we talk about values and our value base, what do we mean? And where do we get our values from? We will now look at this in Activity 2.1.

Activity 2.1

Write down five important values that you feel you have.

Comment

You might have identified that values such as respect, honesty and valuing people are important to you. You might have been told that you are a good listener, or someone who your friends feel they can talk to. You may also belong to a group or community, which may be important, for example, this may provide an identity, friendships and the importance of moral conduct. By moral conduct we are referring to a common set of behaviours, a discipline, certain expectations in which to act and the manner in which we treat other people.

Where do we get our values from?

If we are saying that values are based on an individual's beliefs or principles, then where do we get our beliefs and principles from? These are intangible therefore, we must have acquired them. This is usually during childhood through socialisation, parents, wider family members, friends and the community in which we live. We are taught right from wrong, how to be polite, courteous and respectful. School provides a further element in relation to how children present themselves. Community groups and employment all contribute to reinforcing those beliefs and principles in which we act, or as Goffman (1959/1990) observes, as discussed Chapter 1, we perform. When we talk about Goffman's notion of 'performing', it could be suggested that we are merely performing to an audience. During any given day we could be performing to a wide variety of audiences. Therefore, does this mean that we can perform to all those different audiences with a different set of values? Is this what we mean by a 'value base'? Or does 'value base' refer to an individual's 'core' set of values. Are these core values what we look for or like in other people? Do some people have values we aspire to? We will now look at this in Activity 2.2.

Activity 2.2

When we talk about people having values, what do we mean? Think of someone you know, a family member, a friend, someone you work with, and write down three sentences about their values.

Comment

Within your sentences, could you identify any beliefs or principles? For example, how do they treat people? What do they believe, for example, I believe that all pet owners are friendly. Maybe your friends have similar values such as the importance of being there to support each other.

Our values

Think of Activity 2.1 are these your core values? Are these personal values, and if so, what are your cultural values and community values? Likewise in Activity 2.2 how you described the individual, would you say that they had a core set of values? When we start to explore values, we can see that they are very important and can inform the basis of any relationship, being part of a group and ascribe to the group's values or community values. We have already noted how values are intangible but play an important role in how we treat people, how we behave and how we present ourselves. In the previous chapter, we explored tacit knowledge, 'gut feelings', and how these feelings may inform our behaviour or how we approach people. We could now ask ourselves: is tacit knowledge based on our value base? Or is it based on our experiences? Or both? For example, see Case Study 1.

Case study

As a social worker, you are undertaking an assessment. You arrive at the family home and two adults invite you into their home. You immediately observe three puppies and that the floor is wet. You are invited into the room and asked to sit down.

(Continued)

(Continued)

- How are you feeling?
- At this initial stage what are your thoughts?

You observe a baby and a three-year-old playing with toys on the floor.

- Have your feelings changed and what are your thoughts now?

Comment

The purpose of this Case Study is to get you thinking about how your values might influence how you are feeling and inform your practice. What were you thinking on the way to the family? When you arrived did you observe the garden? How did it look? For example, immaculate, tidy or unkempt? What do these words mean, and how do you define such words in relation to a garden, and from whose perspective? Did this initial observation immediately paint a picture of what the inside of the home might be like? Regarding the two adults who invited you into their home, did you observe their appearance? The way they spoke to you? How they presented? On entering the family home, your initial thoughts might have been associated with the puppies and how you feel about, and your experiences, of dogs or pets in general. The floor was wet; the children were playing on the floor. Your observations are all very important, and will be discussed in more detail in Chapter 7. Consider Activity 2.1, and your five values. Consider whether these values play a part in how you communicate, respond to and interact with adults and children, and whether these observations form part of your assessment. Thus, the question to be asked is, would your assessment be based on feelings, tacit knowledge, experiences or facts?

Do values inform our decisions?

There are many questions to consider, if, when, how and what. However, there is very little information in the Case Study about the family home, the adults, the children and the puppies. Nevertheless, there is a lot of information that could be gained through our observations. When these are added to our feelings, values, beliefs, knowledge and experiences you can begin to see the complexity of undertaking assessments and subsequent decision making. Might how we express ourselves, whether verbally or non-verbally, influence the manner in which we work with the family or assess their needs? Do we believe that puppies should be, or should not be, in a family home when there are children? Such a belief could be based on our childhood experiences, our adult experiences, our family or cultural perspective. As a social worker, do we allow such a belief to inform our practice? This final point raises another important question. If we believe that puppies should not be in a family home where there are children, but the puppies are not presenting a risk, does this, present an inner conflict with our value base? Our personal values maybe such that dogs should not be in the family home. In contrast to what is often referred to as 'professional values', which sometimes conflict with our personal values, for example we may not believe that puppies should be in homes with children. However, if there is no evidence to suggest that the puppies are a risk to the children, what do we do? In Chapter 1, we talked about confirmation bias and in this Case Study would we be searching for the evidence to confirm that the puppies should not be in the family home with the children. Could this be regarded as a fair assessment?

Activity 2.3

Thinking about values and social work practice; write down your answers to the following questions:

- Why are values important to social work practice?
- How do values inform social work practice?
- What underpins our social work values?
- How do we demonstrate our value base?
- How do we use values to reflect on our practice?

What do we mean by ethics?

There are many different kinds of ethics, here we have identified four types:

- Meta-ethics – questioning moral values;
- Descriptive ethics – exploring the understanding of sociology, psychology and anthropology, for example, how individuals behave;
- Normative ethics – relating to moral standards and what is reasonable behaviour and morally right, which is determined by the individual, family, community and society;
- Applied ethics – the pragmatic approach to determining what is right or wrong, examining, evaluating and reasoning. Therefore, there is an element of critical thinking, ethical decision-making and judgement.

Exploring ethics

Social work is usually associated with moral conduct – what is right and wrong. When we talk about moral conduct, we can refer to three classical ethical perspectives: deontology, virtues and consequentialism. Exploring these a little further, the focus of deontological theories is the duties or rules that we ought to be following. For example, duties and rules may refer to social customs such as the duties of a mayor or rules afforded through belonging to an organisation. Duties and rules can also apply within a legal context (Johns, 2020). In contrast, virtue theories relate to moral character, such as personal attributes or dispositions. Consequentialism, also referred to as utilitarianism, places importance on the consequences on one's actions. Here we could explore the consequences of an individual's actions if they were to steal a car. Stealing a car is illegal and morally wrong and the consequences could be wide ranging. Consider the following.

1. The owner may not be able to go to work following the theft or they may be late for work because of making alternative arrangements.
2. The owner may not be able to visit their partner in hospital or attend their health appointment.
3. The owner is a surgeon, who is unable to get to work.

The consequences of not having a car may appear at first glance as being an inconvenience; however, does the inconvenience change in significance in number three?

Social work practice and ethics

When we look at the four types of ethics, and the three perspectives, we can identify significant areas such as moral conduct, what people do and how they treat people, what is right and wrong, specific duties an individual might have in a given role and reasoning: the rationale informing their decision-making. We can identify these areas in the PCF, for instance domain – Values and Ethics, BASW's Code of Ethics (2021) and in the Professional Standards. Let us have a closer examination of the Code of Ethics in relation to social work practice in Activity 2.4.

Activity 2.4

Go to the British Association of Social Workers (BASW) website and look at the Code of Ethics for Social Work (2021). Can you identify what we have discussed above within the Code of Ethics?
Can you identify what we discussed above within the PCF?

Comment

You might have identified that social workers have a responsibility towards their moral conduct. How a social worker presents, works with, and treats people, which all form part of their behaviour or how they present themselves. How the social worker presents could be determined by their personal attributes and dispositions. Such attributes and dispositions form part of the social worker's habitus (Bourdieu, 1977) and will be explored in Chapter 3. Social workers should respect, challenge and apply ethical reasoning to their judgements and their decision making. Additionally, consider how the social worker manages conflicting and competing situations and circumstances, empowers and supports in addition to working within a legislative framework. Also, consider the value base of both the social worker, and the individual they are working with, and how such values might influence their working relationship. The environment in which they are working might also influence the working relationship. Here we can see the interconnectivity between the individuals, but also between individuals and environments (Bronfenbrenner, 1979, 2005, discussed in Chapter 3) including organisational structures.

Ladder of inference

I would like to introduce the ladder of inference. The model, based on human response, was developed by Argyris (1982) and (Senge et al., 1994). The model explores how our actions might be informed by our beliefs. Adapting this model and illustrating through a series of steps we can see how this could be the case.

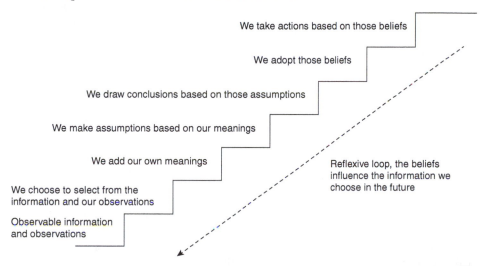

Figure 2.1 Ladder of inference

Source: Adapted from Argyris (1982) and Senge et al. (1994).

The ladder of inference is a tool that could be used to explore how our beliefs can inform our actions and interactions. Illustrating the ladder through a series of steps, Figure 2.1 shows how we start with our observations and experiences. Such experiences might be our own first-hand experiences, but also what we might adopt or adapt from other sources for example our parents, wider family or friends or alternatively what we read, observe or discuss. This could also include government and media representations. All information and observations have the potential to inform our beliefs, or as Butler (1996) refers to, acts as a stimulus. The second step is the selection process where we select aspects of the information from our observations, readings and discussions. Following the selection process we add our own meanings, for the third step, which leads us to the fourth step showing how assumptions can be made from those meanings.

From those assumptions we draw conclusions, this being the fifth step, and subsequently we adopt those beliefs. These beliefs then inform us about the world. They become our adopted truth; knowledge which our actions are based upon. Let us consider the ladder of inference, within the context of social work, through a research summary.

Research summary

Teenage pregnancy and teenage motherhood are identified as a health and social problem (Public Health England, 2019; Social Exclusion Unit, 1999). The predominant discourse is that teenage pregnancy and teenage motherhood is a problem and focuses upon, and emphasises, that the young mothers lack formal educational qualifications, are from and likely to remain, single parent families and whose children exhibit anti-social behaviour. Teenage mothers are typically referred to as having undesirable lifestyle characteristics, an inability to parent their children and are welfare dependent and a drain on society. These young women are problematised and vilified, for example, Duncan (2007, p. 309) writes how young mothers are 'typically, … described as a "toll", "disaster", or a "crisis"'. Whereas Macvarish (2010, p. 2) explains how they are perceived as a 'symbol of social decline, social failure or social backwardness'.

Comment

We can observe from the above Research Summary that teenage motherhood is identified and portrayed as a problem; they are seen as being welfare-dependent and a drain on society. The general public read and listen to these stories and for many individuals these stories are interpreted as the facts, a reality, and therefore are accepted as the truth. Such information informs their beliefs and subsequently assumptions are made. They may also know of someone or have heard of someone locally who is a teenage mother and this might reinforce their beliefs. Within the ladder of inference this is the first step: observable information. From these stories, individuals select information and add their own meanings. We can then see how assumptions might be made based on those meanings and, therefore, we could draw conclusions based on those assumptions, such as all teenage mothers are a problem. Consequently, all young women who are pregnant, or have children, are stereotyped. Stapleton (2010, p. 10) suggests that 'the pervasiveness of stereotyping practices is such that young childbearing women are routinely scripted to become welfare dependent, inadequate mothers of unruly children who, in turn are destined to repeat the cycle'.

What can we learn from the above?

When we consider the above Research Summary and Comment, one question to be asked is: 'is the predominant discourse a factual representation of all teenage mothers?

Are all teenage mothers a problem?' Such a perspective places all teenage mothers as a homogenous group irrespective of their education, socio-economic status or ethnicity. Further, there is no consideration as to whether they are single, living with a partner or married. We could also note that the journey to motherhood is not included. You can begin to see how the identification and portrayal of teenage mothers as a problem is one dimensional. However, this one-dimensional perspective is sensationalised by the media. How the media represents something often influences how people then attach meaning to what they are reading or hearing. From this they make assumption, draw conclusions and adopt these as the truth. Thus, all young women with children are a problem.

The potential impact of the one-dimensional perspective

There is the general assumption that young women, or women who are perceived to be 'young', and seen with children, are the mothers of the children. There is no consideration that the children may be siblings, nieces, nephews or friends' children. Maybe the young women are working as childminders, nannies or carers. The assumption is simply that they are teenage mothers and thus labelled and stereotyped. Such labels and stereotyping contribute towards the stigmatisation and discrimination of young women who are also mothers (Ellis-Sloan, 2014; Fearnley, 2018; Neill-Weston and Morgan, 2017; Wenham, 2016).

Labels, stereotyping and inferiorisation

Let's reflect on what we have discussed in relation to the Case Study so far, we have observed that young women who are seen with children are labelled as teenage mothers. Teenage mothers are seen as a problem. The label 'problem' results in them being stereotyped. Labels can be problematic and judgemental; for example examining labels and roles, McKie and Callan (2012, p. 55) observe that 'the terms teacher, parent and doctor might all suggest roles and responsibilities that promote social cohesion while the terms junkie, thief or teenage mother can create identities that are hard to loosen from associated negative connotations'. The distinction between 'parent' and 'teenage mother' is clear in relation to how teenage mothers are perceived. They are placed alongside the 'junkie' and 'thief', which clearly indicates their position within society in contrast to, and contradictory to, the 'parent' who is acknowledged to have status akin to the teacher and doctor. Here we can begin to recognise the social and moral themes attached to teenage motherhood.

When we consider this in a little more detail, we can see that 'junkie' and 'thief' are often associated with moral character and here we can identify both values and ethical principles that were discussed earlier in this chapter in addition to the act of criminality. We could also say that they are deviant, 'deviance is defined as violations of norms or departures from social expectations' (Lemert, 1972, p. 13). This situates young women who are also mothers as deviant. When we introduce the notion of deviance there are other possible implications, for example this could explain why many young mothers experience hostility (Ellis-Sloan, 2014; Fearnley, 2018; Neill-Weston and Morgan, 2017; Wenham, 2016). Additionally, this could explain why they 'have become the targets of marginalisation and stigmatisation' (Wilson and Huntington, 2005, p. 59). We can begin to see the potential impact of labels, labelling and being labelled. The marginalisation of individuals could lead to social exclusion, social disadvantage and social inequalities.

Stigmatisation

Another consideration is the relationship between labelling, stereotyping, stigmatisation and power. Link and Phelan (2006) identify five interrelated components:

- people identify and label human difference,
- stigma involves the process of stereotyping in which the labelled person is linked to undesirable characteristics,
- the group doing the labelling separates 'them' the stigmatised group and 'us',
- stigmatised people experience discrimination and loss of status,
- the exercise of power.

(Link and Phelan, 2006, p. 528)

Link and Phelan's (2006) five components illustrate how a combination of factors contribute not only towards the stigmatisation of individuals, but also labels them as undesirable and situates them as 'others', and thus power can be exercised. Examples of such are where they live, the welfare benefits they receive and the places they are able to socialise, or feel able to socialise. Such stigma also impacts on an individual's life chances (Link and Phelan, 2006). Therefore, we can see not only how labelling individuals might contribute towards a multiple array of social inequalities but also injustice. Additionally, here we might want to consider the importance of the PCF domain – Rights, Justice and Economic Well-being.

As we explored above, if young mothers are placed in the same category as a 'junkie' or 'thief', they may be regarded as discredited or to have a blemished character (Goffman, 1959/1990) They are discredited because they have not conformed to the socially constructed normative feminine expectations of, firstly, a married woman and, secondly, a mother (Wilson and Huntington, 2005). We could therefore consider a blemished character due to the assumptions being made about their marital status and moral conduct. Lemert (1972, p. 68) suggests that 'the concept of stigma is burdened with certain archaic connotations suggesting tribal exclusion of unspecified provenience'. These 'archaic connotations' may correspond with the historical discourse in relation to the unwed mother and associated stigma attached to illegitimacy (Wilson and Huntington, 2005).

Inferiorisation

Further to this discussion, Adam (1978, p. 9) draws our attention to deviance and its relation to inferiorisation by asserting that '*deviance* is a normative term which glosses or suppresses the social construction of stigma and obscures the essential aspect:

inferiorization [original emphasis]'. Adam (1978, p. 43) goes on to say that for any given category of the 'inferiorized' there is a composite portrait which is founded on three axioms (1) a 'problem' (2) all alike, and (3) recognisable as such'. We can recognise these three axioms within the identification and portrayal of young mothers as a problem, identified as all the same, the assumption that all young women with children are mothers.

Drawing on the historical discourse, the contextualisation of young mothers as a problem is not a new phenomenon (Bainbridge, 2009). The difference being that historically, having a child outside of wedlock was seen as a serious offence (Schur, 1984). When we take into consideration the sociohistorical factors such as the social positioning of motherhood and associated discourse in relation to the unwed mother: 'unmarried motherhood in our society is looked on as the violation of cultural norms' (Bernstein, 1974, p. 101). The portrayal of young motherhood as a problem is reminiscent of the historical unwed mother whereby having a child out of wedlock was a moral issue, a moral issue that required addressing. Here we see the connection with normative ethics – relating to moral behaviour as discussed previously in this chapter.

Activity 2.5

Previously in this chapter we discussed four types of ethics. We can see from above the connection between young mothers and normative ethics can you identify any connections between the other three types of ethics and young motherhood?

The ladder of inference in practice

The ladder of inference is, as suggested, a tool to explore how assumptions, based on our beliefs and associated meanings, inform our perspective of certain aspects of the world. We can see how easy it is to subscribe to the one dimensional 'problematisation' discourse associated with teenage motherhood. As social workers we need to ask ourselves whether the decisions we are making are informed by our beliefs or assumptions. Let's consider our practice by firstly critically evaluating the predominant discourse and secondly being aware of how such discourse informs our practice. When working with individuals, for example young women who are also mothers, we could explore their journey to motherhood and listen to their story. Here we can begin to see how the ladder of inference can be used as a tool to question our beliefs, assumptions and how these might influence our value base.

Exploring labelling

Labels are attached to many individuals for a variety of reasons including the clothes they wear. For example, individuals who wear clothes with hoods attached are frequently referred to as 'hoodies'. This identity is often associated with young people although there have been many media stories relating to individuals from babies to the elderly wearing hoodies. Nevertheless, it is young people who are frequently labelled, stereotyped and stigmatised. These young people wear clothing, usually because of fashion or identity, a sense of belonging, or both and are often stereotyped as troublesome – a problem. However, how many other people wear such garments and are stereotyped in the same way? Nevertheless, the label 'hoodies' typically refers to young people who are unemployed and not in education, employment or training (NEET). Let's think about labelling through the following two activities.

Activity 2.6

Thinking about labels that are attached to different individuals – children and adults, create a list of twenty labels.
Thinking of these labels how many have positive connotations? How many have negative connotations?

Comment

You might have thought of labels relating to disability, culture, identity and sexuality. Another example of labelling might have been a reference to a child who is 'naughty' or 'clever'. What do these labels mean? How do such labels impact on individuals?

Activity 2.7

Thinking about your list of labels in Activity 2.6, what impact do you think the label might have on the individual. For example, someone who is given the label of 'beautiful', 'fat' or 'clumsy'.

Comment

The attached label could increase or decrease confidence, self-esteem or could make an individual feel self-conscious. Here we could see how labels could have an impact on individuals resulting in anxiety in relation to body image, eating disorders, mental ill health or disengagement from school or further education. Subsequently, the individual acquires multiple labels, such as 'fat', 'eating disorder', 'mental health' and 'truancy'. You can see how labels can be accumulated, and this thus raises the question of whether labels contribute towards an individual's identity, if that identity is a chosen one, and does the individual behave in a manner in which they believe they should act.

Stereotyping

Another example of stereotyping is the portrayal of black men, some of whom also wear hoods. A visual campaign documenting 56 black men's narratives illustrates 'I am Not My Stereotype'. Cephas Williams, the founder of the campaign, says he is tired of how people look at him when he wears his hoodie 'I am a black man with a degree in architecture, and I find I am not taken seriously when I walk into a room full of strangers' (Freeman-Powell, 2019). All of the 56 men are either entrepreneurs or are in employment.

Implications of labelling and stereotyping

The three examples, teenage mothers, young people who wear hoodies, and black males, and all examples of individuals who are labelled, stereotyped and stigmatised. There are many other individuals who are placed into groups, homogenised and subsequently marginalised and discriminated against. Moral judgements can be made through our communication, language used and the labels we ascribe. What identifies other individuals as being different from ourselves? Thornicroft et al. (2007, p. 192) suggest stigma is 'an overarching term that contains three elements: problems of knowledge (ignorance), problems of attitudes (prejudice), and problems of behaviour (discrimination)'. The question to be asked is: are the individuals, in the three examples, treated fairly and with respect? Consider our previous discussion, and the activities completed previously about values, especially how values play a part in how we communicate, respond to and interact with individuals. Also let's consider whether these people are treated ethically. Again, we could refer to moral rights and how people can be expected to be treated. Here we could consider the Human Rights Act 1998 and the Equality Act 2010 (Johns, 2020).

Activity 2.8

Thinking about how these individuals are treated; write down your answers to the following questions:

- Why do think the individuals, identified above, are treated as they are?
- Do you think that an individual's values play a part in how they are treated?
- Considering the four different kinds of ethics, discussed previously, which one do you feel is the most relevant?

Cultural humility

Within social work there are many terms of reference with regards to culture and working with different cultures, two such terms are culture awareness and cultural competence. Such terms would suggest that we, as social workers, need to be aware of every culture or alternatively be competent working with every culture. However, it would be very difficult to have an awareness, knowledge and understanding of every culture. The question to be asked is what do we mean by culture? Johnson (2013) highlights that there were at least 150 definitions of culture between 1920 and 1950. This illustrates the complexity of what is meant by culture, but also of the many interpretations. Culture is associated with the arts, there is popular culture and some communities are distinguished by their culture. In the 1970s, culture began to emerge within sociology and explored the concepts, understanding and meanings of 'culture, cultural difference and cultural conflict' (Spillman, 2020, p. 12). Contemporary notions of culture 'emerged in Europe as a way of characterising differences between human groups, and changes within them … what we would now call cultural difference' (Spillman, 2020, p. 7). Therefore, when we talk about cultural awareness and cultural competence, we need to be explicit, but how can we be explicit when there are so many different meanings?

When we talk about cultural awareness and cultural competence, within social work, we are usually referring to diverse populations and cultural differences, which returns us to our previous observation, and acknowledgement, that we cannot be aware of, and have knowledge and understanding of, every culture. Additionally, there are differences between and within cultures. Therefore, we are at risk of homogenising cultures and individuals within those cultures. We need to be aware of, and recognise, individual identities and different cultural identities. We need to respect and celebrate difference. According to Fisher-Bourne et al. (2015), cultural humility is an alternative to cultural competence. Self-reflection is crucial to cultural humility and therefore, there is a need to examine our own attitudes and beliefs on issues of power, privilege and diversity. Here we can see how the ladder of inference could be a useful tool to self-examine our beliefs and attitudes, and reflect on their appropriateness. Through these reflections we increase our own knowledge and understanding of how our beliefs and attitudes might impact on individuals along with raising awareness of our own biases and stereotyping. Additionally, there is the need to challenge institutions, inherent structural factors and inequalities and injustice. Table 2.1 provides a comparison of cultural humility and cultural competence.

Table 2.1 Comparison of cultural humility and cultural competence

	Cultural competence	Cultural humility
Perspective on culture	• Acknowledges the layers of cultural identity • Challenges stereotypes • Difference is seen in the context of systemic discrimination	• Acknowledges the layers of cultural identity • Recognises that working with cultural differences is a lifelong and ongoing process • Emphasises not only understanding the 'other' but understanding ourselves as well
Assumptions	• Assumes the problem is a lack of knowledge, awareness and skills to work across lines of difference	• Assumes that in order to understand clients, we must also

(Continued)

Table 2.1   (Continued)

	Cultural competence	Cultural humility
	• Individuals and organisations develop the values, knowledge and skills to work across lines of difference	understand our communities, colleagues and ourselves • Requires humility and recognition of power imbalances that exist in client–provider relationships and in society
Components	• Knowledge • Skills • Behaviours	• Challenging power imbalances • Institutional accountability • Ongoing critical self-reflection
Stakeholders	• Practitioner (primarily)	• Practitioner • Client • Community • Institution/Organisation
Critiques	• Focus on knowledge acquisition • Issues of social justice not inherent • Regarded as a 'cookbook' approach • Leads to stereotyping the 'other' • Suggests an endpoint	• Lack of empirical data • Lack of conceptual framework

Source: Fisher-Bourne et al. (2015, p. 172).

Self-questioning

vThere are many times when we need to ask ourselves: why did we decide to do that? Or ask others: why did you decide to do that? And you will most probably find that the answer is because we have always done it that way. Through self-questioning and reflection, we can explore whether 'that way' is the best approach, the most appropriate method, but there might be alternative approaches and methods of doing something. We therefore need to question ourselves and others about why we do certain things in certain ways. In order to gain an understanding of individuals and different cultures we need to ask questions and it is through questions such as: Could you help me to understand? Could you tell me more about your culture? We gain an understanding of what culture means to individuals, to families and communities. Let's explore their journey, listen to their stories and discover new meanings rather than refer back to old beliefs and assumptive ideas. Self-questioning, explorative questioning and reflection are essential skills in social work, but also in everyday life.

Activity 2.9

Revisit Activity 2.1, write down five important values that you feel you have. Considering a self-questioning, explorative questioning and reflective approach, why are these five values important to you?

Table 2.2 provides us with some questions to explore cultural humility from an individual and organisational perspective.

Table 2.2 Individual and organisational questions to assess cultural humility

	Essential questions for critical self-reflection	Essential questions to address power imbalances
Individual-level	• What are my cultural identities? • How do my cultural identities shape my worldview? • How does my own background help or hinder my connection to clients/communities? • What are my initial reactions to clients, specifically those who are culturally different from me? • How much do I value input from my clients? • How do I make space in my practice for clients to name their own identities? • What do I learn about myself through listening to clients who are different than me?	• What social and economic barriers impact a client's ability to receive effective care? • What specific experiences are my clients having that are related to oppression and/or larger systemic issues? • How do my practice behaviours actively challenge power imbalances and involve marginalised communities? • How do I extend my responsibility beyond individual clients and advocate for changes in local, state, and national policies and practices?
Institutional-level	• How do we organisationally define culture? Diversity? • Does our organisation's culture encourage respectful, substantive discussions about difference, oppression and inclusion? • How does our hiring process reflect a commitment to a diverse staff and leadership? • Do we monitor hiring practices to ensure active recruitment, hiring and retention of diverse staff? • Does our staff reflect the communities we serve? • Is our leadership reflective of the populations/communities we serve?	• How do we *actively* address inequalities both internally (i.e., policies and procedures) and externally (i.e., legislative advocacy)? • How do we define and live out the core social work value of social justice? • What are the organisational structures we have that encourage action to address inequalities? • What training and professional development opportunities do we offer that address inequalities and encourage active self-reflection about power and privilege? • How do we engage with the larger community to ensure community voice in our work? What organisations are already doing this well?

Source: Fisher-Bourne et al. (2015, p. 176).

Activity 2.10

Look at Table 2.2, consider our previous discussion about values and ethics and their importance in building relationships. Now identify three goals that you could do to increase your knowledge and understanding of working with individuals.

Activity 2.11

Again, look at Table 2.2, what three things could organisations do to promote equality.

Values and ethics: implications for social work practice

Professional practice

As social workers our behaviours and actions have the potential to improve people's situation and therefore can be described as having a 'positive outcome'. Conversely, our behaviours and actions have the potential to damage and do harm and therefore can be described as having a 'negative outcome' (Oko, 2011, p. 40). In Chapter 1, we explored professionalism, the importance of communication and having an underpinning knowledge base and here we begin to see how values and ethics are significant within social work practice. Oko (2011) identifies five areas of interrelated factors to consider:

- the influence of our personal values and their impact on our practice,
- our view about the nature and purpose of social work,
- professional values and professional codes of ethics and practice,
- the influence of ethical theories in determining how we ought to behave as professional social workers,
- components of ethical decision-making.

(Oko, 2011, p. 40)

Within the above, we should consider BASW Code of Ethics for Social Workers (2021), which outlines values and ethical principles such as human rights, social justice and professional integrity along with ethical practice principles. There are also the UK's four professional bodies, SWE – Professional Standards; Wales – Practice Guidance; SSSC – Codes of Practice for Social Service Workers and Employers; Northern Ireland – Standards of Conduct and Practice for Social Workers (see Table 1.1, Chapter 1) which a social worker needs to adhere to. You can now begin to gain an understanding of how we treat individuals might be a moral consideration, but also is embedded with social work practice.

Activity 2.12

Go to the British Association of Social Workers (BASW) website and identify the Code of Ethics for Social Workers (2021). Then go to Chapter 1, Table 1.1, and identify the areas that relate to values and ethics within the Professional Standards.

- What similarities are there between the Code of Ethics and the Professional Standards?
- What words are used that refer to values?
- What sentences describe ethical practice?

Comment

The purpose of this activity is for you to familiarise yourself with what is expected of a social work student and a social worker, what represents good social work practice and the importance of treating individuals with respect, dignity and integrity. You might have identified similarities such as rights, responsibilities, trust and have recognised how importance is placed on working with individuals, maintaining and developing relationships and gaining their confidence. Additionally, there is the promotion of their health, well-being and independence. These areas correlate with Chapter 1 and being a professional.

Social work practice

There are many challenges to social work practice and working with individuals. We need to be aware and recognise that some individuals might not wish to work with us, welcome us or be courteous towards us. It is difficult not to personalise some of these actions and reactions, but we need to remember that such reactions are because of the 'social work' and subsequent role and responsibilities of the social worker. There are also challenges within children and families social work and in particular areas such as child protection. Consider how might a social worker work anti-oppressively, or apply respect and dignity to someone who has, or is, abusing a child or another individual. Once again, we can see the importance of communication skills (see Koprowska, 2020, working with involuntary clients). There are no easy answers, but as social workers we need to remain professional, follow the professional standards and ensure that we are working within ethical guided principles. This may appear to be an idealistic and simplistic perspective; however, when working with individuals, we can, and should, treat them with respect, dignity and gather factual evidence to enable the law to be applied juristically. In Chapter 1, we began to identify the foundations of professional social work practice – see Figure 1.5. We will now add our values and ethics in Figure 2.2.

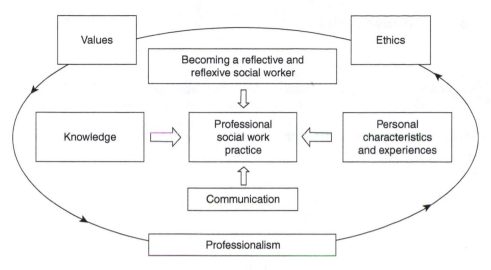

Figure 2.2 Building on the foundations of professional social work practice

When we add values and ethics to our model of good practice, we can see the multiple dimensional aspect of good practice that is underpinned by professionalism, value and ethics. This is the foundation for social work practice that facilitates an open and honest approach without prejudice from our beliefs or assumptive considerations and an ethical approach that includes reasoning and a rationale for the decisions that we make. As social workers, we make these decisions following listening to multiple voices, a diversity of voices, and through the engagement of individuals. Through a thorough understanding of the purpose of our involvement with children, adults and families, and the ability to articulate the purpose of our involvement in a clear manner, considering language and presentation, we are able to negotiate, communicate and make decisions and professional judgements based on fact and supported by evidence.

Activity 2.13

Take a look at Figure 2.2 and then go to the PCF on the BASW website. Make a list of how many of the PCF domains you can identify?
Go to Table 1.1 Chapter 1, can you identify any of the Professional Standards in Figure 2.2?

Before we draw the chapter to a close there are three more things I would like you to consider. Firstly, communicative ethics; secondly, narrative ethics; and thirdly, how we apply values and ethics to the digital world. By digital world, I am referring to emails, messaging and social media. These are a form of communication, and as discussed in Chapter 1, we need to act in a professional manner, we need to be digitally responsible (Taylor, 2017).

Communicative ethics

Communicative ethics relates to the relationship between history, culture, language and performance; as Witkin (2017, p. 41) asks 'how do we do ethics in our dialogical encounters'. An example to illustrate this is the language used to describe teenage mothers. However, when we reflect on such discourse, we can begin to see that there are institutional structures preventing them from moving away from this position. There are few opportunities for them to move away from being welfare dependent because of the lack of affordable childcare that would enable them to engage in further education or employment. The question to be asked here is whether the language used is oppressive. We will explore language in such circumstances in Chapter 4. Additionally, we could consider whether teenage mothers are oppressed because of the barriers and inequalities that prevent them from becoming independent. As social workers we can reflect on, and challenge, our practice, but can we challenge institutions as within the principles of cultural humility? We need to listen and observe how language is used, we need to ask questions and challenge labels, and challenge institutional practices that oppress individuals: 'the traditional approaches to moral conduct … deontological, consequentialist, and virtue – provide the philosophical underpinnings of social work ethics' (Witkin, 2017, p. 40). However, moral conduct changes over time and therefore we need to ask ourselves if it is fair to apply a historical moral conduct to the contemporary landscape of what we define as a family or how we treat individuals based on their culture or appearance. As social workers we should listen to their story, to gain an understanding of their lives and communicate in a language that does not oppress, but rather empowers. Here we could consider the dramaturgical approach to reflection discussed in Chapter 1, and reflect on the language we use to engage and describe individuals.

Narrative ethics

Narrative ethics relates to stories, how these stories are told, and by whom, and the relationship between the storyteller and the listener – the family telling the social worker. The retelling of these stories could change the context of the original story depending on how it is told, the language used, and how it is expressed. As a social worker, listening to a child or parent, we might retell their story in many different ways. For example, recording their story in case notes, assessments and reports and during supervision, during conversations with colleagues, other professionals and through the giving of evidence in court. Therefore, we need to be aware of how we communicate their story. We need to consider the words we use, the labels we ascribe to their situation and circumstances, and ask ourselves; is this an accurate and true reflection of their story? We therefore need to listen carefully, clarify our understanding and choose our words carefully when retelling their story ensuring accuracy, respect and integrity. Here we could reflect on the dramaturgical approach to reflection discussed in Chapter 1, and in particular how we edit their story.

Values and ethics in the digital world

Any chapter on values and ethics needs to consider the digital world. Here I would like to talk about two significant considerations. Firstly, how we communicate in the digital world on a personal level and how we communicate on a professional level whether through emails of via social media. The two are intertwined simply because of our digital identity. You might post on social media and think that it is 'personal' or that it has a short lifespan. However, someone may see the post and repost it to another social media site or screenshot it and place it on another platform. Therefore, it could be argued that whatever you post on social media has the potential to be permanently visible and available for anybody to see. You may not want a prospective employer to see your holiday photographs or read about a good night out with friends. Also consider the words, language and communication. Within a professional capacity you need to adhere to the PCFs, but also the Professional Standards. BASW has a Social Media Policy and the Professional Standards incorporate social media. Within a professional capacity give consideration to your emails. They need to be professional in their context, you need to consider the language used and not to use abbreviations. The recipient needs to be able to understand what you are saying or asking. Whether as a student or qualified social worker, you need to familiarise and adhere to the agency's Use of Electronic Equipment policy. Some employers might have a different name for this policy. This policy usually includes the use of mobile telephones, the internet and accessing information. Think about values and ethics, what are your values and what might be the consequences of that email or social media post?

Secondly, we live in a digital world of connectivity and accessibility, and in which we are always available. Often, we work from home and work at home. We therefore need to be conscious of our health and well-being and apply self-care skills. This includes taking regular breaks, exercise and ensuring that where we are working is comfortable with regards to positioning, seating and the use of the computer. We also need to consider who is in the room, what digital equipment we are using, what we are sharing and where we are storing information and ensuring confidentiality. Importantly, we need to switch off, at the end of the working day and at weekends unless the service provision is providing out of hours services. Again, think about self-care.

Values and ethics in a digital world summary

- Familiarise yourself with the Professional Standards – England, Scotland, Wales and Northern Ireland – use of social media,
- Familiarise yourself with the BASW Social Media Policy,
- Identify your placement provider's/employer's 'Use of Electronic Equipment Policy' and apply it in practice,
- Communication – remain professional, consider words, language and actions and interactions,
- Social media – apply values and ethics to all social media posts,
- Take care of yourself – familiarise yourself with, and develop, self-care skills.

Chapter summary

In this chapter, we have started to explore the meaning of social work values and ethics. The explorations and discussions have made links to becoming a professional and professional practice. Values and ethics were considered in relation to relationships with other people in addition to making decisions. You explored the ladder of inference and how this might be used as a tool to explore how beliefs, assumptions and subsequent actions can be based on those beliefs and assumptions. The Research Summary provided you with the opportunity to consider values, ethics, beliefs and assumptions in addition to the potential impact of labelling. The two further examples continued the discussion with regards to labelling along with stereotyping. Following our explorations of labelling and stereotyping, we explored cultural awareness, cultural competence and cultural humility. The implications for social work practice then became the focus and where we reconsidered the discussion relating to the preparation for professional practice. The chapter drew to a close by exploring communicative ethics, narrative ethics, and values and ethics in the digital world. The next chapter will consider two theories and their relevancy to social work practice along with exploring the interconnectivity between individuals and individuals and the environments they live, engage and visit.

Further reading

Banks, S (2021) *Ethics and Values in Social Work*, 5th edn. London: Red Globe Press.

This book provides a critical discussion of ethical issues, problems and dilemmas in relation to relationship-based approaches to social work. This includes exploration of professionalism and codes of ethics and ethical judgements and decision-making.

Witkin, SL (2017) *Transforming Social Work*. London: Palgrave.

This book explores a wide range of social work theories, approaches and perspectives. The chapters 'Revisioning Social Work Ethics' and 'Difference, Noticing, and Cultural Competence' are particularly useful and will build on your knowledge gained from this chapter.

Useful website

BASW: https://www.basw.co.uk/about-basw/code-ethics.

3

Theories for practice

(Continued)

5.1 During their qualifying degree studies in social work, students acquire, critically evaluate, apply and integrate knowledge and understanding in the following five core areas of study.

5.2 Social work theory

See Appendix 2 for a detailed description of these standards.

Introduction

We have identified in the previous two chapters that social work is underpinned by knowledge and that knowledge can be gained in many different ways. We have also established that values and ethics play a significant part in relationship building along with decision-making. In this chapter, you will be introduced to two theoretical constructs. Firstly, Bronfenbrenner's ecological framework and secondly, Bourdieu's conceptual tools of habitus, capital and field. We will explore these two theoretical constructs in relation to social work practice with the focus on working with children and families. Building on your knowledge gained in Chapter 1 relating to becoming a critically reflexive social worker, you will explore these theoretical constructs in relation to yourself, your relationships with others, and how these theories can be applied in social work practice.

The ecology of human development

The ecology of human development (Bronfenbrenner, 1979) is a framework for exploring the relationship between a person, their microsystem, and the environment in which they live. We will explore the microsystem later in this chapter. Firstly, let's consider what we mean by the ecology of human development:

The ecology of human development involves the scientific study of the progressive, mutual accommodation between an active, growing human being and the changing properties of the immediate settings in which, the developing person lives, as this process is affected by relations between these settings, and by the larger contexts in which the settings are embedded.

(Bronfenbrenner, 1979, p. 21)

Let's explore this quotation further. You can see that importance is placed on the interactions between individuals and their surrounding environments in relation to human growth and development. For example, individuals interact with their immediate family members, such as those within their own household, along with wider family members, friends and work colleagues. Interactions within different environments might include the community in which they live, school or work. Here you can see the interplay between the individual interacting with other individuals within the environments they frequent, all of which could influence the level of interaction.

Activity 3.1

Consider the following scenarios: what are your initial thoughts in relation to how the interactions might be influenced by

- the relationship between the individuals
- the environment in which the interaction takes place.

Also consider the potential impact of the interactions on the individual's development.

Dora and Serlina are friends. They have known each other for many years. Today they are meeting in one of their favourite coffee shops and discussing their shared interest in gardening.
Kevin, the manager, is having a meeting with Jason, IT operator, who inadvertently pressed a wrong key on the computer and deleted a major piece of work.
Mia (mother) and Antonio (father) are sharing Hilda's (daughter) excellent school project work feedback, from her teacher, with Hilda's grandparents. Hilda is very happy to talk about her project.

Comment

Within these scenarios we can see how the different relationships and environments can influence the interactions. For example, Dora and Serlina would appear to be relaxed and comfortable with each other's company. They are sharing their experiences of gardening which could contribute towards their development. Whereas, Kevin and Jason's discussion might not be relaxed or comfortable. The discussion, depending on Kevin's communication skills and ability to articulate the consequences of Jason's error, while at the same time not to undermine his abilities, has the potential to negatively impact Jason's confidence and subsequent development. For Hilda the experience is a positive one. This includes positive feedback from her teacher, parents and grandparents all providing Hilda with praise and encouragement. This is likely to impact Hilda's confidence, the sharing of her work increases her knowledge and understanding of the work completed, all of which contributes positively towards her development.

Activity 3.2

Think about your interactions, for example your communication and engagement, with family, friends and within the community, how have these interactions influenced your development?

We can observe from Bronfenbrenner (1979) and Activity 3.1 and Activity 3.2 that an individual's development does not occur in isolation but through a great number of interactions and experiences. The ecological framework enables the social worker to see how an individual's internal world is intertwined with their outer world. The core of Bronfenbrenner's (1979) ecological framework is a set of nested structures, which are referred to as the microsystem, mesosystem, exosystem and macrosystem. The ecological framework was later developed and incorporated four interrelated components. This was referred to as the 'process-person-context-time' (PPCT) model (Bronfenbrenner, 2005):

- **Process** is the developmental process of the individual.
- **Person** relates to the biological, cognitive, emotional and behavioural characteristics of the individual.
- **Context** includes the four nested systems: the microsystem, mesosystem, exosystem and macrosystem.
- **Time** can be described as multidimensional, for example human growth and development time, family time, time with friends and historical time. The time component is referred to as the chronosystem.

Exploring the PPCT model further, we can see that the 'process' component refers to the development process. This includes theories of human growth development across the lifespan including biological, psychological and sociological aspects (Parker and Ashencaen Crabtree, 2020; Walker and Horner, 2020). The 'person' component refers to the characteristics, predispositions and demeanour of the individual, their personality, including how they present themselves and respond to others. This could also include identity, sense of belonging, how we see ourselves and the relationship we have with the wider society (Elliott, 2020). The 'context' component refers to the four systems:

Microsystem – within the microsystem, the individual is at the centre of the system and directly interacts in, and influences, numerous microsystems. This is usually described as immediate family members – those living in the same household. Bronfenbrenner's (1979) framework defined the microsystem as:

A microsystem is a pattern of activities, roles and interpersonal relations experienced by the developing person in a given setting with particular physical and material characteristics.

(Bronfenbrenner, 1979, p. 22)

This was later amended to:

A pattern of activities, social roles, and interpersonal relations experienced by the developing person in a given face-to-face setting with particular physical, social, and symbolic features that invite, permit, or inhibit engagement in sustained, progressively more complex interaction with, and activity in, the immediate environment.

(Bronfenbrenner, 1994, p. 1645)

Within the later definition, Bronfenbrenner (1994) expanded on the original in recognition of the changing and developing world. Here we can see how the significance of not only the face-to-face interactions with individuals, but also symbolic interactions are included. Additionally, we can see how some interactions also hinder engagement, for example the scenarios discussed previously. Here we see Dora and Serlina's interactions are fluid, with both of them engaging in their shared interest. Whereas, Kevin and Jason's interactions might be less engaging and more constrained. This will depend on a number of factors including their relationship and how they communicate, navigate and negotiate the mistake made. We can begin to see how individual's microsystems are influenced and impacted upon by others. Since Bronfenbrenner amended his definition, the world has changed significantly and is continuing to evolve and develop. We need to recognise and acknowledge the significance of technology and in particularly the internet. For instance, social media plays a significant part of everyday life and incorporates many of the patterns of activities that Bronfenbrenner (1979/2005) refers to, with the exception that these activities are virtual, online experiences, which could include face-to-face, but the difference being that the individuals might not be in the same room or geographical location. The activities might be online, and not within the immediate environment, for example a family home, but this raises the question of what do we define an environment to be? Within the family home we could be online and having a virtual face-to-face discussion with family members in another area of the UK or in another country. Such a discussion could be influential in the individual's development. Take for example Hilda's grandparents who live in Italy, but their praise and encouragement could have a significant bearing on her development.

Mesosystem – the mesosystem is the relationship between two or more microsystems. For a child it could be within their home and school, and for their parent it could be within home and their place of work. Mesosystem is therefore several interacting microsystems. Consider the potential number of interacting microsystems for a child at home, such as child/parent, child/sibling. This continues for each parent and each sibling; thus there are a multitude of interacting systems at play.

Exosystem – where two or more microsystems interact within one environment and whereby another environment directly connected with one individual might indirectly impact or influence another individual. For example, a parent's employment will directly impact on the parent but will also indirectly impact on the other family members. The actions of the employer might indirectly impact on, for example the child. Think about the consequences of the parent being made redundant. This would affect the parent, but also the child through the changing financial circumstances. An example might be the potential impact on the child – they can no longer participate in activities with friends and consequently become isolated. The exosystem is also influenced by changes within the macrosystem.

Macrosystem – this is the prevailing ideology within which the individual and their microsystem, mesosystem, and exosystem operate together in the wider social, political and economic environment. This could include, for example a change in the welfare benefit payments. Once again, we can see how a change in welfare benefits would have a direct impact on the parent and indirect impact on their children.

Within each system, the individual is continually evolving and the action and interactions within these systems are fundamental to their growth and development.

The family is a functional system and the day-to-day aspects of family life are changed by its internal composition and external forces (Bronfenbrenner, 1979).

Chronosystem – 'the chronosystem model: its design permits one to identify the impact of prior life events and experiences, singly or sequentially, on subsequent development' (Bronfenbrenner, 2005, p. 83). Such life events or experiences could include the changing or maturing body or the impact of external factors. Let's fast forward 20 years where we see Hilda reflecting on her school experience and in particularly the feedback she received from her teacher and subsequent encouragement from her parents and grandparents. Hilda was thinking how this encouragement had contributed to her academic confidence which she feels enabled her to develop and progress in her chosen career. This is an example of prior life events and experiences and the impact thereof over time.

Ecological framework – ecologies of self

The ecological framework applies to each family member and thus each individual will have their own ecologies of self. These ecologies will be interacting with other family members in addition to extended family members, friends and other individuals they come into contact with. The interconnectivity between these numerous relationships influences and impacts each other. Therefore, each parent will have their own ecosystem, likewise each child, and these ecosystems will be influencing and impacting on each other. Such interconnectivity between these relationships will initiate different responses from each individual, parent/child, and will be determined, to some extent, by the parent's habitus, and the child's developing habitus. This will be discussed further next.

Activity 3.3

Thinking about Bronfenbrenner's ecological framework, write down your answers to the following questions:

- How much do you think the environment influences your relationships? For example, where would you meet a friend, and why in that environment?
- A close friend has received negative comments about their new haircut from one of their friends who you do not know. How do you feel?
- You have known a friend for ten years; how has your relationship changed over that time?

Bourdieu: habitus, capital and field

Another theoretical construct I would like to introduce to you is Bourdieu (1977, 1984, 1990, 1991). Bourdieu's conceptual tools of habitus, capital and field are of importance for social workers in a number of different ways. For example, in their most basic presentation they provide the social worker with an overarching portrait of an individual's life. We will explore each area further within this chapter. Firstly let's consider this portrait.

Habitus

Habitus is the inherent set of enduring internalised predispositions, characteristics and attributes of an individual. This includes accent, mannerisms, and presentation in social situations (Bourdieu, 1984). It is these features that contribute towards the way an individual thinks, feels, judges and acts in certain predetermined ways gained from societal conditioning and socialisation (Bourdieu, 2003). Here we could consider theories of human growth and development (Parker and Ashencaen Crabtree, 2020; Walker and Horner, 2020) where parenting and the home environment are the predominant factors of socialisation and societal conditioning during infancy and childhood (Bourdieu, 1977). Additionally, there are wider family members and friends, along with the community and schools all of whom play an important part. Their perceptions, values, feelings and predetermined responses and frames of reference define their world. Frames of reference may include, for example, language, culture, ideology and paradigms. Children gain a construct of associations through their experiences including family and community along with the transition to adulthood and continues throughout their lives. Habitus can be described as a multitude of features that are inherent to an individual's character along with the social structure that is embedded within all of us and which influences our ways of interpreting the social world. Here we can make reference to the ladder of inference, explored in Chapter 2, and consider where our beliefs and assumptions might originate. We can use the concept of habitus to gain an understanding of how individuals are a complex fusion of their past and present (Bourdieu, 1990).

These predispositions play a significant part in an individual's life chances. Life chances are determined, according to Bourdieu (1977), by the individual's habitus as it becomes embedded in their articulation, values and beliefs, how they act and engage within the sociocultural aspects of everyday life including the choices and the activities in which they participate. Habitus is not a fixed entity and as such new experiences within the social context can introduce different social norms and therefore individuals can exercise choice and agency over habitus, although there may be limitations. An individual's habitus can influence how they adapt or innovate in response to situations as they arise. Therefore, it could be argued that habitus influences and is influenced by the social world.

Capital

When we explore what is meant by capital, in relation to Bourdieu (1977, 1984), we can see that it means possessing certain attributes, characteristics, knowledge, status, or wealth. Bourdieu discusses four types of capital: cultural capital, social capital, economic capital and symbolic capital. Together these four sources of capital represent advantage and disadvantage in society. Bourdieu's (1984) cultural capital involves an individual's possession of recognised knowledge and is fundamentally a relational concept. Therefore, it cannot be understood in isolation, but in conjunction with other forms of capital. The four types of capital are:

- Cultural capital – the accumulation of knowledge, behaviours and skills and other cultural acquisitions. Cultural capital represents non-economic factors such as family, commitment to education and social class and therefore, could relate to the individual's social status and social mobility.
- Social capital – an individual's social network. This also includes networks of support and influence. This includes family, friends, engagement within the community and group membership.
- Economic capital – material wealth such as financial, property and other assets.
- Symbolic capital – socially recognised and sanctioned prestige or honour.

These different forms of capital can enable access to, or possession of, a range of different types of resources. These resources can be material, cultural or social. The social hierarchy of an individual in society will be determined by the amount of, and type of, capital possessed. However, capitals could be significantly different for different individuals (for example see Thatcher et al., 2018).

Activity 3.4

Identify and write down examples of different types of capital you have in your personal life.

- cultural capital
- social capital
- economic capital
- symbolic capital
- How did you develop these forms of capital?
- Now consider how you will develop your capital as a social worker?
- How could these sources of capital inform your social work practice?
- How will these forms of capital enable you as a social worker to be resourceful?

Comment

Through your reflections of how you developed these different forms of capital, how did you think your knowledge and skills could be transferred to social work practice? For example, cultural capital could be gained through your academic studies and placements, social capital through meeting different social workers and other professionals thus building your networks. This could increase your knowledge and understanding of social work practice and in turn increase your cultural capital. Following completion of the social work course and gaining employment will contribute towards economic and symbolic capital, but also culture capital through social mobility. Here we can see the interplay between the four capitals.

Field

Field represents the social and institutional places and spaces or networks where an individual may be socially positioned. Within these places, spaces and networks, an individual's habitus is developed and embedded, for example the home, school, community and work environment. Children are socialised to family mores and norms and it is through this socialisation that they are introduced to 'networks' of family members, friends and associates. As children develop and transition to adulthood, their capital is developed and built upon as they become acquainted with, and develop, their own networks. As individuals we compete for various types of capital within the field in order to improve our positions. It is this competing that is characterised by power disparities (Bourdieu, 2003).

Bourdieu's (2003) interpretation of field can be social, cultural, educational, religious, artistic, economic or intellectual and are invariably hierarchical. Each field will have its own guiding principles, implicit and explicit rules of conduct along with policies and procedures. The interrelationship between these various practices, an individual's habitus and access to, and possession of, capital are all determinants of where they are situated in the field; 'one of the most important properties of fields is the way in which they allow one form of capital to be converted into another in the way, for example, that certain educational qualifications can be cashed in for lucrative jobs' (Bourdieu, 1991, p. 14). However, such social mobility is not always possible (Friedman, 2018) in addition to organisational structures and what Friedman (2018) and Laurison (2020) refer to as 'the class ceiling'.

Symbolic power

Symbolic power does not refer to a specific type of power, but rather an aspect of power that is usually deployed in social life:

> If one wishes to understand the ways in which symbolic power is exercised and reproduced in our societies, one must look more carefully at how, in different markets and fields, institutionalized mechanisms have emerged which tend to fix the value accorded to different products, to allocate these products differentially and to inculcate a belief in their value.
>
> (Bourdieu, 1991, p. 24)

Symbolic power is generally in representative form as opposed to the exercise of physical force. Therefore, symbolic power carries a legitimacy that it would not otherwise have: 'symbolic power has to be based on the possession of symbolic capital'

(Bourdieu, 1990, p. 138). For example, to call yourself a social worker, you need to hold a recognised qualification and be registered with Social Work England (Social Workers Regulations, 2018). Therefore, as a social worker you hold symbolic power by the very nature of the qualification, registration and possession of the title. When considering symbolic power, we also need to think about communication in its many guises, for example verbal and non-verbal behaviour including language, words, symbols and how they are used. The organisation that employs the social worker with its policies and procedures, status and recognition exercises power over the social worker and communities where individuals live, and the government exercises power through legal frameworks over the organisation, social worker and society.

Symbolic capital and symbolic power

As discussed previously, symbolic capital is the socially recognised and sanctioned prestige or honour. This might include formal educational qualifications, a certain employment position or a position of power held within a group. Symbolic power refers to the exercise of power within that position. Let's consider the following scenario: Gina is a social work student who upon completion of the social work degree secures employment as a Child and Family Social Worker. The qualification, registration and employment contribute towards her symbolic capital. Gina's career progresses and she is successful in her application for the position of Director of Safeguarding for a Local Authority. Here we can see how Gina's social capital, in addition to all the other forms of capital, contribute towards gaining the prestigious role of Director. As Director, Gina can exercise symbolic power, for example, through the creation and implementation of the Safeguarding Strategy. Here you could revisit Chapter 2, Table 2.2 Individual and Organizational Questions to Assess Cultural Humility, and think about how Gina might answer the questions, on an individual level and an institutional level, to address the power imbalances and promote equality and diversity.

Applying the two theoretical constructs in social work practice

The application of Bronfenbrenner and Bourdieu's theoretical constructs will be explored through the notion of family life. The family is a functional system, where relationships are inextricably interwoven, and the operation of which is fluid due to both internal and external forces. Each adult family member has their own habitus and capital along with their respective fields. The children will have developing habitus and capitals. Through Bronfenbrenner's PPCT, and Bourdieu's conceptual tools, it can be seen how each family member is influenced by, and influences, the experiences within the home environment, but also the community and wider society. The family functions in more than one ecology, for example personal, community, school or work. The child's development incorporates a variety of experiences through parental, wider family and friend's engagement and activities and the integration of their formal education. Here we see an interplay between the four interrelated components within the ecological framework (PPCT) (Bronfenbrenner, 1979/2005), in addition to Bourdieu's (1977, 1984, 1991) concepts of habitus, capital and field.

When these two prominent sociological constructs are applied in social work practice, they enable the social worker to gain a greater understanding of the complexities of the individual's relationships with other individuals (children and adults) and the various environments they engage within. Additionally, the social worker is able to identify support networks, protective factors and risk factors in addition to how the wider social, economic and political aspects might be impacting upon each family member and the family collectively. Additionally, when other theories, models and perspectives are taken into consideration, and applied in practice, the social worker can gain a deeper understanding of each individual, and the family's world. Table 3.1 provides an overview of some of the links that could be made.

Table 3.1 Linking Bronfenbrenner and Bourdieu with associated theories

Bronfenbrenner	Bourdieu	Link to
Process • child development • development through the life course	Habitus • internalised dispositions • characteristics • attributes	Human growth and development theories. Theories of identity.
Person • characteristics • cognitive • emotional • behavioural		Sociological theories such as symbolic interactionism and social constructionism
Context • microsystem • mesosystem • exosystem • macrosystem	Capital • cultural capital • social capital • economic capital • symbolic capital Field • school • community • work • social/leisure	Context, Capital and Field can also be linked to theories of human growth and development, along with gender, class, ethnicity, social policy, politics Field – community psychology, social psychology, sociology, social policy
Time (Chronosystem) • current time • historical time • family time • time with friends • time to socialise		Time – the overarching element that covers all aspects of human growth and development through the life course which can be reflected upon and divided into elements of time

Consider a child's habitus

Let's think about this: habitus is the characteristics, internalised dispositions, and attributes of an individual. Therefore, we could say that a contributory factor in the child's developing habitus is the interactions within their microsystem, the interconnectivity between the individuals, and the environment, in which they live, attend school and play.

However, there are factors that influence the child's habitus, for instance parental employment which has an indirect impact on the child – the exosystem. You could consider the wider political and economic factors – the macrosystem, for example when a parent has become unemployed. You can see how the child's habitus could be influenced by a family with a secure, stable, and what could be described as a comfortable home environment. However, as a consequence of wider socio-economic factors, the child's home environment could become fraught with anxieties, insecurity and uncertainties. This is where you could explore theories of human growth and development (Parker and Ashencaen Crabtree, 2020; Walker and Horner, 2020), identity (Elliott, 2020) and social policy (Dean, 2019) all of which would increase your understanding of working with children and families. The questions to be asked are what impact would this loss of employment have on the child; and would the impact be short or long term. The impact might also be positive. For example, if the parent's employment involved working long hours with many days working away from home, they would have much more time with their child. The loss of income may be temporary and local employment sought.

Think about the following two scenarios and complete Activity 3.5.

- A parent has significant social capital, a wide social network of friends and acquaintances. Their economic capital is secure. They have a variety of assets to draw upon. The parent shares their news of impending unemployed within their networks and drawing on their capital are able to secure employment without loss of income.
- A parent has very little social capital. They are reliant on employment being advertised. Usually this is low paid and often insecure. This is another period of unemployment and therefore they have not been able to build their financial capital.

Activity 3.5

Thinking about the two scenarios above, what might be the potential impact on the child?
Consider the home environment, education, leisure activities, along with their development, health and well-being.

Personal lives, family lives

Each family member's identity is intersected with the multiple identities of their personal lives along with their various roles, expectations and competing demands. They are expected to negotiate and navigate these diverse geographies. The competing demands placed on the family challenge their ability to manage their lives. Their personal micro-system may temporarily be disrupted through circumstances such as health, bereavement or unemployment. The relationships, within their systems, may have an influence, or impact, on their children, for example family functioning, family adaptability and cohesion. Family conflict may arise as a result of added stress. Family members and friends may be a significant source of support but also stress. They are expected to manage all aspects of their everyday lives within their respective fields. Within each field there are competing structural demands, macro influences and symbolic power. Again, they are expected to negotiate and navigate these aspects of everyday life.

Applying the two theories to social work practice

Applying these two theories to social work practice is twofold. Firstly, reflecting on your own PPCT (Bronfenbrenner, 2005) and habitus and capitals (Bourdieu, 1977, 1984), you are likely to gain a deeper understanding of yourself in addition to a greater awareness of how your relationships are intertwined with your inner and outer worlds. Through self-exploration and reflection, you can become more aware of, and recognise the importance of, your available capitals and how these were developed, along with your positioning within any given field. This understanding of self and the impact of self on others will be explored through the lens of becoming a critically reflexive social worker, which will be explored further in this chapter, and build upon your understanding from Chapter 1. However, before we explore becoming a critically reflexive social worker, let's look at a Case Study and complete Activity 3.4. We will then explore the second reason for adopting Bronfenbrenner and Bourdieu's theoretical constructs.

Case study

Betty has been reflecting on where her values have come from and has realised that many emanated from her childhood and the strong family values that surrounded her as a child. Betty recognised that she comes from a loving home where there were members of the community who provided a sense of belonging and contributed to her development. Betty describes herself as being confident within her own family and surroundings, but also recognises that she lacks confidence in relation to her education. This lack of confidence, she believes, holds her back. Reflecting on her relationships, Betty has five children and a supportive family, along with some good friends. She recognises the interrelationships between immediate family members, extended family members, friends and the wider community, all of which provide her with a sense of belonging and security. Betty is aware that the wider social, economic and political areas influence, and have an impact, on her family and friends, their prosperity and their health and well-being in addition to their community. Over time, Betty has accepted that there are things she cannot change, for example her time as a child and

(Continued)

(Continued)

living in poverty, which impacted on her education and playing with friends. However, she feels this enabled her to develop resilience. Betty acknowledges that her characteristics and predispositions have all contributed towards her confidence depending on the situation and circumstances. Betty has a strong sense of identity. She has built her capital including social networks such as family, friends and within the community, economic capital through employment and symbolical capital through her various volunteering and employed positions.

Activity 3.6

Betty's reflections demonstrate an awareness of the ecological framework including process, person, context and time (PPCT) (Bronfenbrenner, 2005) along with habitus, capital and field (Bourdieu, 1977, 1984, 1990).
How would you describe Betty's understanding of self in relation to the ecological framework and habitus, capital and field?

Secondly, by applying these theories in practice, you are likely to gain a deeper understanding of the lives of the children and families you are working with including exploring their various relationships within, and external, to the family home. Through such an approach, along with an understanding and application of other theories, models and perspectives, your practice will be underpinned by a theoretical framework that will enable you to gain an understanding of the multiple perspectives of individual lives. Before we explore this further, read the Case Study and complete Activity 3.5.

Case study

In the previous case study, we saw Betty reflecting on her personal life. Here we see her reflecting on her role as a children and families social worker. Betty qualified as a social worker eight years ago and immediately gained employment in a Children with Disability Social Work Team that works alongside the Disability Family Support Team. The two teams work with children and young people with disabilities. Betty supports social work students on placement and newly qualified social workers undertaking their ASYE. Betty works with many children and young people with complex needs, their parents and wider family members. In addition, she also facilitates a support group for siblings of children with disabilities. Betty works in collaboration with colleagues from health and education along with many other professionals and therefore, has built a network of colleagues who she can draw upon for support, resources and information.

(Continued)

Betty enjoys her social work role, is proactive in advocating on behalf of families and is a member of a national group raising awareness about families with children with disabilities.

Activity 3.7

Betty's experience as a social worker illustrates how the ecological framework including process, person, context and time (PPCT) along with habitus, capital and field is applied in practice.

- Can you identify the various aspects of the ecological framework and habitus, capital and field in relation to Betty's social work practice?
- Considering the PPCT, how does Betty present herself in her social work role in comparison to her personal life?
- Considering the four types of capital, can you identify any examples of Betty drawing on her capital in her social work role or personal life?

Comment

As you are reading through these two Case Studies and Activity 3.6 and Activity 3.7, you might have identified similarities and differences between various aspects of the ecological framework and habitus, capital and field in relation to Betty's personal life and professional role. For example, think about Betty's confidence in both her personal life and professional role, and although she says she lacks confidence in education and feels this holds her back, she is a qualified social worker, and supports students and newly qualified social workers. She is also an active member of the community and an active member of different groups supporting families with children with disabilities. Here we see Betty drawing on her capital, whether this be her 'personal' sources of capital in relation to her own family, friends and community involvement or 'professional' sources of capital including networking, facilitating groups or supporting individuals.

Becoming a critically reflexive social worker

In order to illustrate the significance of applying Bronfenbrenner's and Bourdieu's theoretical constructs to social work practice, reflexivity, discussed in Chapter 1, will be explored: 'reflexivity is a well-established theoretical and methodological concept in the human sciences, and yet it is used in a confusing variety of ways. The meaning of "reflexivity" and the virtues ascribed to the concept are relative to particular theoretical and methodological commitments' (Lynch, 2000, p. 26). Cunliffe (2004) suggests focusing on three areas:

Existential: Who am I and what kind of person do I want to be?
Relational: How do I relate to others and to the world around me?
Praxis: The need for self-conscious and ethical action based on a critical questioning of past actions and of future possibilities (Jun 1994).

(Cunliffe, 2004, p. 408)

Let's consider these three areas: Firstly, **existential** – who am I and what kind of person do I want to be? Consider Betty in the two case studies. What kind of person do you think Betty is? Do you think she knows who she is? When you read about Betty, there is a strong sense of belonging: she talks about family, friends and the community. She engages in various groups and projects, and all of these aspects are important to her. As a social worker she supports others, facilitates groups and advocates on behalf of others. Betty presents herself as someone who has a strong value base, a self-awareness and comfortableness of her own position.

The second area, **relational** – how do I relate to others and the world around me? Betty presents herself with a sense of self-awareness. She appears to be well aware of her own ecologies of self, her own communication – verbal and non-verbal, body language and how she can influence others. There is evidence of reflection when she notes how she lacks confidence in relation to education and this holds her back, yet she is able to support others with less experience. She is well aware of her symbolic power through her qualification and employment status and uses this in a proactive way to advocate and support others and this is evident in both her personal life and involvement in the community and also within her professional role.

The third area, **praxis** – the need for self-conscious and ethical action based on a critical questioning of past actions and of future possibilities. Betty provides examples of this within her personal life and professional role. Through reflection, she highlights family values, childhood, education, and how all these areas have contributed towards a sense of who she is, a sense of belonging, what is important to her and how she draws on these aspects to inform her personal and professional roles. There is evidence that Betty has many sources of capital, family, friends and involvement in the community but also, she uses this knowledge and understanding of the importance of capital to inform her social work practice. This is evident through supporting others, proactively advocating on behalf of others and engaging in a national group to represent the families she is working with. All of which is drawing on, and developing, her many sources of capital, which she is using, along with all aspects of her ecologies of self, to inform an ethical based practice.

Self-awareness

We can begin to understand the difference between reflection and reflexivity through how Betty reflects on her personal and professional roles. Reflecting on her roles and experiences, she demonstrates reflexivity through her self-awareness of how her presence, communication and emotions along with her beliefs and assumptions influence and impact on others. Such self-awareness, knowledge and understanding will contribute towards your developing relationships with others, in addition to understanding how you engage, participate and work with children, parents and families. Becoming a critically reflective and reflexive social worker facilitates the exploration of the moral dimensions of social work that comprises of recognising and acknowledging your own beliefs and values and the potential impact of such on the decisions and judgements you make. We now have a greater understanding of the interconnectivity between the habitus, capital and field in addition to the relationship between the microsystem, mesosystem, exosystem and macrosystem.

The critically reflexive social worker

Becoming a critically reflexive social worker is invaluable in developing, building and maintaining relationships. As you become aware of your ecologies of self, your self-awareness, and insightfulness of who you are and want to be, you will gain a deeper understanding of how these aspects impact on relationships. With experience you will develop an understanding of how different characteristics, attributes and experiences influence, inform and impact on the lives of individuals and professional practice. How you communicate and the manner in which your communication is delivered can evoke emotional responses. Emotions can also impact the development and maintenance of relationships. Furthermore, a key aspect of the social worker's role is to recognise and acknowledge diversity, in addition to being supportive, encouraging and critically analysing multiple perspectives of both micro and macro landscapes. Applying these two theoretical constructs in practice is significant in relation to how you interpret, understand, observe and interact with individuals.

Implications for social work practice

Let's consider child development, parental support networks including wider family members and friends, socialising and employment. You can begin to see the relevance of Bronfenbrenner's four interrelated components of the PPCT along with Bourdieu's concepts of habitus, capital and field. Through the lens of these theories, you could identify the characteristics, attributes and values of individual family members, along with their various sources of capital and available resources. You could explore the family composition and interplay between the multidimensional relationships in addition to wider structural factors. This would enable you to gain an understanding of the historical, situational and contextual factors of individuals' lives. Gaining such an insight into individual family member's PPCT and habitus, capital and field could inform the social worker's practice, assessment and intervention. Assessments will be explored further in Chapter 7. Importance should be placed on getting to know the family through explorative discussions and discovering their journey and listening to their narratives. Here you can see the relevance and significance of communicative and narrative ethics as discussed in Chapter 2. By having a greater understanding of the family, you can identify their strengths, needs and risk factors in addition to providing focused support. Additionally, recognising and acknowledging the power imbalance between yourself and the family is essential. Further, developing trust is crucial to empowering the family and creating an understanding of the purpose of your involvement while at the same time recognising and acknowledging that when working with a family, you become a part of each family member's microsystem. Additionally, when undertaking assessments, you need to be aware of the complexities of individual and family lives that are subsumed within the wider political, economic and social factors. The interplay between the individual and structural factors should be identified and explored along with any possible marginalisation, inequalities and injustice. Here you are developing an understanding of what a social worker should know, the significance of professional standards and the relevance of social work values and ethical practice.

Working with change

Additionally, the 'field' (Bourdieu, 1984, 1991), for example home environment, community, work or school, may consist of hierarchies relating to symbolic power both individually and structurally. Through the development of your assessment skills and working collaboratively with the family, along with other professionals, the impact of micro and macro changes can be identified and thus interventions become more purposeful. Communication and interpersonal skills are essential in relationship building. These areas were discussed in Chapter 1 and Chapter 2.

Let's consider relationships through the theoretical constructs of Bronfenbrenner and Bourdieu. When we talk about relationship building, we are talking about you developing a relationship with each family member in addition to working collaboratively with colleagues and other professionals. The relationship between the four interrelated components referred to as the PPCT (Bronfenbrenner) and habitus, capital and field (Bourdieu, 1977, 1984, 1991) is multidimensional. In one direction, there is the flow of influence from field to the habitus that will challenge your ecology of self in many ways, for example intellectually, your values, and confidence. When we talk about the ecology of self, we are referring to the systems that are intrinsically interwoven within you. In another direction your ecology of self, including habitus can influence the perceptions and experiences of other individuals including family, friends, colleagues and other professionals. Hierarchy is always a potential threat with some individuals feeling that they have higher status, authority or that their values are more important. Here you will need to manage the situation through the application of interpersonal skills, demonstrating knowledge and understanding of the situation, the family's needs, strengths and risk factors, but also, and more importantly, a thorough understanding of the purpose of your involvement.

You may be seen as supportive, but more likely to be seen as intrusive. You are, to the family, a professional, confident, knowledgeable and articulate; additionally, you might be seen as having power. Therefore, it is important to recognise that power is always an integral part of the relationship between any habitus and any field and as such needs to be acknowledged. These aspects, as highlighted previously, are referred to as symbolic power and having an awareness of this power whether perceived or real needs to be considered in relation to how you, the social worker, is seen but also the potential impact this might have on your relationships with the family. Additionally, power needs to be considered because you are assessing the family and therefore there is the potential for an unequal relationship to exist. The word 'potential' is used because the family are the experts of their own lives, with individual members having specific knowledge that you do not know.

You need to apply your knowledge and skills to establish what you need to know to complete a thorough assessment, working in partnership with the family. You also need to consider how your ecologies of self, in addition to your habitus and capital, are informing your practice. Through critical reflection, you can raise your own awareness of how different experiences may influence and inform your practice. This also includes your interpersonal skills, for example how you communicate, how you present and how you engage with different members of the family and other professionals and practice within different situations and circumstances. From a professional perspective, you can reflect on your strengths, such as your communication skills along with identifying areas for development, for example developing your skills of assessing different situations and experiences from multiple perspectives and the need to build your professional networks – social capital (Bourdieu, 1977, 1984). Through critical reflection, you should be considering how your beliefs, values, actions and interactions along with your interpersonal skills might influence your meaning making, professional judgements and ethical decision-making.

Chapter summary

This chapter introduced you to the theoretical constructs of Bronfenbrenner's ecological framework and Bourdieu's conceptual tools of habitus, capital and field. You explored these constructs in relation to social work practice focusing on working with children and families. You developed your knowledge gained in Chapter 1 relating to becoming a critically reflexive social worker in addition to considering Bronfenbrenner and Bourdieu's theoretical constructs. The chapter closed through examining the implications of applying such theories to practice. The theories introduced in this chapter will be explored in the chapters that follow and be related to working with children and families and social work practice. In the next chapter, we will continue the journey of developing our knowledge and skills in relation to working with families.

Further reading

Bronfenbrenner, U (1979) *The Ecology of Human Development: Experiments by Nature and Design*. Cambridge: Harvard University Press.

Bronfenbrenner, U (ed.) (2005) *Making Human Beings Human: Bioecological Perspectives on Human Development*. London: Sage.

These two books thoroughly explore Bronfenbrenner's ecology of human development. They provide a comprehensive explanation of the microsystem, mesosystem, exosystem and macrosystem and the relationship between the developing human being and environment. The initial ecological framework was redefined and developed into the biopsychosocial model which includes all aspects of human growth and development. The four systems identified in Bronfenbrenner's (1979) earlier work was incorporated within the PPCT model.

Bourdieu, P (1977) *Outline of a Theory of Practice*. New York: Cambridge University Press.

Bourdieu, P (1984) *Distinction: A Social Critique of the Judgement of Taste*. London: Routledge.

These two books provide a comprehensive theoretical examination of Bourdieu's conceptual tools: habitus capital and field. They critique social class, examine identity, social space (field) and behaviour. The examination of capitals provides a framework for understanding power and the reproduction of inequality.

Thatcher, J, Ingram, N, Burke, C and Abrahams, J (eds) (2018) *Bourdieu: The Next Generation: The Development of Bourdieu's Intellectual Heritage in Contemporary UK Sociology*. Oxon: Routledge.

This edited book offers different perspectives on Bourdieu's work. The book starts by introducing Bourdieu's concepts. This is followed by each chapter that includes reflection and research on Bourdieu's concepts. This includes diversity, class, gender and inequality. It is a book that provides an overview, insight and also exploration of Bourdieu's concepts habitus, capital and field to real-life situations and circumstances.

4

Working with families

(Continued)

5.4   Service Users and Carers
5.15 Communication Skills

See Appendix 2 for a detailed description of these standards.

Introduction

So far, we have explored professionalism, values and ethics and two theoretical con-structs which all have an emphasis on social work practice. In this chapter, you will develop your knowledge further as we turn our attention to working with families. We will begin by exploring the term 'family'. Through our exploration of the family, we will be looking critically at the functionalist approaches of the family. This will include the notion of the nuclear family, the family structure and how families contribute towards the socialisation of children. The nuclear family was seen as the archetypal family and so we will examine the idealisation of the nuclear family and ask whether this was representative of all families. We then look at how contemporary family formations differ including exploring single-parent families and invisible families. We will begin to look at government policies and initiatives and explore how these have the potential to impact individuals and families. You will develop an understanding of how policies, designed to support families, have the potential to label and oppress them through their use of language and categorisation. This will be followed by exploring how some families and individuals are invisible, but yet visible through labelling. The final section will look at describing family life through family practices and how families display themselves. Firstly, let's consider your perspective of 'family' by completing Activity 4.1.

Activity 4.1

Write down what the word family means to you?
Save your notes for later when we will return to them.

The 'family'

Talk to anyone about 'family' and it engages many different meanings, emotions and memories. The family is made up of relationships between individuals and is related to growth, development and health and well-being along with being intertwined with religious and moral beliefs. The family is also multidimensional and is constantly changing through the dynamic relationship between family and social change. Social change, such as demographic, culture, economic and political actions and interactions, both influences and impacts on individuals and families. Likewise, individuals and families influence social change. One definition of the family is 'a cluster of positions to and through which an individual traces crucial kinship links, particular links with others which give him/her rights and positions' (Keesing, 1976, p. 292). The notion of kinship links could relate to ancestry and places individuals and families within a historical context or alternatively links to family members in other countries. With technology we are not only able to trace our ancestors but also have discussions with, and virtually meet, family members in different parts of the world. In Chapter 3, we explored the ecological framework, and through this framework we can see how kinship links are interconnected. Additionally, within this definition we see how family members have different positions and rights. This is an example of symbolic power as discussed in Chapter 3.

Activity 4.2

Thinking about the definition of the family above (Keesing, 1976), how would you rewrite this for today's families?
Does your definition contain any thoughts or words from Activity 4.1?
Save your notes for later when we will return to it.

Comment

As you can see from the two Activities, we have our own thoughts, feelings and definitions of what a 'family' is. When the microsystem (Bronfenbrenner, 1979/2005) of individual family members is explored, there will be a myriad of different interactions and experiences. Individually and collectively, the lifestyle, ambiance and experiences within the family are, to some extent, influenced by culture, values and beliefs. To some extent, an outside factor, such as employment, is a significant determinant of lifestyle which impacts where one lives and also the experiences within the family home. Here we could consider two contrasting perspectives both resulting in the same impact on family life. Firstly, employment might provide a lifestyle of choice and economic capital (Bourdieu, 1977, 1984), but at the same time be a significant stress factor. Secondly, unemployment might not provide economic capital, choice or material wealth, and the financial constraints might be a significant stress factor. Recognising that stress is a contributory factor of abuse, child abuse and domestic abuse, we can see how employment or unemployment could impact upon the family. There are also other factors that impact on the family such as health and well-being. The macrosystem, as discussed in Chapter 3, impacts greatly on the individuals within the family and therefore, in turn, family life. Consequently, the microsystem and macrosystem (Bronfenbrenner, 1979/2005) are intertwined and experienced through the interplay of cultural and structural factors. It is all of these experiences throughout childhood that are significant in the formation of the child's habitus (Bourdieu, 1977, 2003) and are the foundations of their developing capital (Bourdieu, 1977, 1984), as explored in Chapter 3.

Activity 4.3

Thinking about the inner world of the family and the outer world of community, society and environmental factors, how do you feel these might influence each other and impact on family life?

Functionalist perspective of family

Sociologists have studied families, in the context of the family's role, function and place within society throughout history. In the 1950s, an American sociologist, Talcott Parsons, applied a functionalist perspective using a systems metaphor to demonstrate that families were needed for a harmonious society. The functionalist perspective 'is that everyone has a set position and task in society (function) and that we are all interdependent upon one another in the successful running of society' (Nobbs et al., 1980, p. 9). From both the micro level and macro level, certain roles and responsibilities of individuals within the family and between family members are prescribed: 'the role of husband or wife is prescribed by society, and the relations between them are structured by their mutual expectations as to what constitutes "wifely" or "husbandly" conduct' (Cotgrove, 1970, p. 40). The phrase 'wifely and husbandly conduct' has a historical context and feel and these roles are explored and illustrated eloquently in a study of women, housework and the division of labour (Oakley, 1974/1976). These roles are also seen to be essential to maintaining the social order whereby each family member has a role and responsibility towards maintaining equilibrium within the family and society.

Let's consider the family from the functionalist perspective. From this perspective the family was referred to as the 'nuclear family'. The family structure consisted of two heterosexual adults who were married and had children. As noted earlier, the adults had specific gendered functions. These were the male, the man of the house, who was the breadwinner and provided for the family. The female was the carer who looked after the male and their children. The female contributed towards the children's education and provided emotional support to both the male and their children. The two adults, the parents, socialised their children to the norms and expectations of society along with reinforcing gender-specific roles of masculinity and femininity (Jamieson, 2005). These 'gender roles of "masculinity" and "femininity" may be experienced by people in their daily lives as spontaneous dispositions, but are in fact deeply determined by the wider society and culture' (Elliott, 2009, p. 188). Furthermore, 'gender is bound up with cultural focuses of socialisation, role learning and gender stereotyping' (Elliott, 2009, p. 189). The nuclear family became the archetypal family, demonstrating worth and appropriate values, in addition to preparing children to be the next workforce. Within the functionalist perspective, individuals were categorised, labelled and expected to fulfil their assigned role.

Activity 4.4

What do you feel are the strengths and limitations of the functionalist perspective?

Comment

The ideology relating to the construction of the nuclear family suggests that a family is not formed until a child is born. The formation of a family originates from traditional beliefs associated with relationships: 'the nuclear family is a moral or normative ideal type, an abstraction that captures the essential features of how we think families ought to be' (Gelles, 1995, p. 6). Here we see how the family structure 'ought' to be, giving clear indications of the requirements to what a family should be. There is also reference to traditional values and beliefs along with what is morally acceptable. Such traditional values, beliefs and morals are represented through the nuclear family. Here we can observe the interplay between values and ethics, discussed in Chapter 2, family life and wider society. As you can see, the discourse associated with the nuclear family became firmly established and anything other than that was seen as non-acceptable; '"discourse of the family" wields a power to declare what is normal and what is unacceptable' (Muncie and Sapsford, 1997, p. 10). Such discourses change over time and are influenced by moral values, societal values and the prevailing political ideology; therefore, 'discourse is language used relative to social, political and cultural formation, it is language reflecting social order but also language shaping social order and shaping individual's intersection with society' (Clarke, 2002, p. 10). However, those who did not conform to the notion of the nuclear family were regarded as deviant (Giddens, 2009). Here we see how values and morals play a significant part in determining what is right and wrong, and as discussed in Chapter 2, these aspects are often determined by what we believe. Once again, we can ask where do we get our beliefs from. Here we can see that there could be a historical, societal, political, family or cultural aspect; for example, are young mothers stigmatised for being a 'young mother' or for the perceived notion of 'single motherhood' and not conforming to the nuclear family?

This raises the questions of how does the dominant discourse become just that 'dominant', what are societal norms and who decides such norms? As we saw earlier, the roles of wife and husband were prescribed by society and anything other than that was seen as deviant. However, Becker (1966) raises our attention by noting that individuals who are regarded as deviant may not be. Indeed, they are labelled as such, nevertheless, 'deviance is *not* a quality of the act the person commits, but rather a consequence of the application by others of rules and sanctions to an "offender" [original emphasis]' (p. 9). In other words, individuals who do not conform to being a nuclear family are not necessarily deviant, but seen as such by others. The notion of the nuclear family was also criticised: 'the ideology of the family gives ultimate control to men ... (Hence, the description of the nuclear family as "patriarchal")' (Dallos and Sapsford, 1997, p. 154). Giddens (2009) states that 'the dominance of the traditional nuclear family was steadily eroded over the second half of the twentieth century' (p. 174).

The illusion of the nuclear family

The nuclear family has declined in significance, but as McRobbie (2009) suggests, 'the most demonised category making out an alternative to mainstream family life is that of the "single mother." In UK political parlance this group of women find themselves most consistently vilified' (p. 51). However, the single-parent family is not new; according to Oakley (1976), 'fifty-eight percent of British households were not of the nuclear family type according to 1966 data, and one in twenty of all households is a single-parent family' (p. 9). Therefore, when we explore the ideology of the nuclear family, it can be seen that it was just that, an ideology that served a function at a particular point in history. An ideal, but in reality, not necessarily the norm and prescribed during a time when family structure and formation was changing 'the perceived necessity of regulating unmarried parenthood suggests the fragility of the institution of marriage in the first half of the twentieth century' (Holden, 2007, p. 113). Nevertheless, this illusionary portrayal of families during the post war period continues to exist. Further, the portrayal continues to be represented in both literature and films whereby the unmarried mother conflicts with the social norms of marriage:

> By tracing the different ways in which unmarried motherhood is represented in these films and novels, it is possible to identify how a complex web of relationships between marriage, singleness and motherhood was constructed and given meaning in the period's structure of feeling. These relationships are shown to be mutually constitutive, with the character of the unmarried mother standing as a motif for understanding not only the experiences of having a child outside marriage but also what it might mean to be a married woman.
>
> (Fink, 2011, p. 156)

The difference between the married and unmarried woman in popular culture once again illustrates how the construction of family, and in particular the married woman, was represented. Furthermore, 'unmarried women were constantly judged against the standards of their married counterparts' (Abrams, 2002, p. 99) and to some extent continue to be within contemporary society. Once again, we can see values and morals at play. Evans (2011) reminds us that 'the structure of family life that many people believe to be new since the 1960s – cohabitation, many births outside marriage and transient family relationships – have a much longer history' (p. 48). Not only did the women experience stigma of being a single parent, but also the 'Bastardy Acts' continued to be in place until 1987. These Acts gave children born outside of marriage fewer rights than those within. Although there is more acceptance of single parents in society today, stigma continues to exist.

Activity 4.5

Do you think single mothers are stigmatised? And if so, why?

Research summary

According to Gingerbread, in the United Kingdom:

- There are around 1.8 million single parents – they make up nearly a quarter of families with dependent children.
- Less than one per cent of single parents are teenagers.
- Around 90 per cent of single parents are women.
- The average age of a single parent is 39 years.

(Gingerbread, 2019)

Towards contemporary notions of family

The changes that occurred during the 1960s and 1970s had significant effects on family structures and family diversity. Indeed, since that time, families have become more diverse and increasingly include single parents, step-parents, same-sex parents and multiracial parent families. Some two parent families live apart, as single parents, but regard themselves as a family. Family can also include extended family members and sometimes individuals are referred to as family when there is no biological or marriage connection. According to Williams (2004), 'the only difference is that today's "new family forms" are yesterday's immoralities' (p. 70). In the twenty-first century, the notion of family has changed in formation and composition; however, the basic premise of two adults living together remains the same and is synonymous with traditional values and beliefs. When considering the notion of family, we need to ask whether a family needs to consists of children, or can two adults be a family? Or maybe one adult living alone? Maybe one adult with their relationships with other individuals being online? This takes us back to thinking about what is a family along with the diversity of family formations.

Activity 4.6

How many different family formations can you think of?

Comment

Thinking about different family formations, did any of these formations align with how you described the family in Activities 4.1 and 4.2?

Activity 4.7

Let's explore these family formations further; search for UK Government policies on family within the last 10 years. This search may include government and non-government websites, research, or the independent, voluntary or private sector. However, focus on government policies. What words are you going to use, how are you going to describe the family and what needs to be included for you to consider a policy to be on family?

When looking for family policies, observe how families are portrayed, the words used to describe families and the focus of the policy.

Government policies

England – The Troubled Families programme (2012–15).

The programme conducted targeted interventions for families experiencing multiple problems, including crime, anti-social behaviour, truancy, unemployment, mental health problems and domestic abuse.

A Manifesto to Strengthen Families – Policies for a Conservative Government to strengthen families.

The programme aims to support up to 20 local authorities to improve work with families to safely reduce the number of children entering care. This will be achieved through a number of projects. These projects aim to enable more children to stay at home in safe and stable family environments, so that fewer children need to be taken into care. They will do this by strengthening local practice systems to more effectively meet the needs of children, developing services that build resilience in families and enabling social workers to manage risk more confidently, so children can stay safely within the home.

Scottish Government – The Scottish Government: The Children and Families Policy Map includes child protection, youth justice, poverty and social justice, early education and childcare, looked after children, human rights, getting it right for every child, and maternal and child health.

Welsh Government – Families First: Programme Guidance (2017)

Families First is designed to improve outcomes for children, young people and families. It places an emphasis on early intervention, prevention and providing support for whole families, rather than individuals. The programme promotes greater multi-agency working to ensure families receive joined-up support when they need it.

The intention of the programme is to provide early support for families with the aim of preventing problems escalating.

Northern Ireland – Early Intervention Transformation Programme (EITP), March 2014–March 2020

This programme provided support to families through early intervention and evidence-based approaches with the focus on the following four workstreams:

Workstream One: Funded four projects across health and education to equip all parents with the skills, knowledge and confidence to give their child the best start in life.

Workstream Two: Funded one project across five different geographic areas across Northern Ireland to support families when problems first emerged before the need for statutory involvement.

Workstream Three: Funded 13 projects across the care system, public law proceeding and justice to positively address the impact of adversity on children and young people.

Workstream Four: Funded one project to strengthen the culture of inter-professional working practice with a particular focus on trauma informed practice.

Activity 4.8

How are families represented within these policies?
What language is used?
How are they described?

Comment

A commonality within these policies is how some families are represented as being in need of intervention, protection and support. They are represented as being a family that is typically unemployed, lacking in formal education and who exhibit anti-social behaviour. The construction of knowledge, surrounding these families, is intertwined with the process of othering. The position of the 'other' is usually assigned to groups of people, often unemployed or without formal educational qualifications and who are frequently blamed for their unwise life choices, or unexpected life events, which usually result in detrimental consequences. However, we need to ask ourselves, who is creating such policies? Who determines the 'other', and that somehow a lack of formal qualifications equates to a need for intervention? Also, the question here is about education and why individuals are leaving school without qualifications. There are many jobs that do not require formal qualifications. However, many of these jobs are asking for qualifications and therefore exclude individuals who would otherwise be suitable candidates. Additionally, although unemployment is falling, it is 'individuals whose parents were in working class roles [that] are still more likely to be unemployed than those whose parents were in professional roles' (The Social Mobility Commission, 2019, p. 14).

Here we can make reference to Bourdieu's (1977, 1984) capitals, which illustrates how some individuals have different capitals or have not had the opportunity to develop their capitals during childhood; 'cultural capital is appropriated through the home environment' (Bowers-Brown, 2018, p. 59) and maybe their home environment did not provide the opportunity. Additionally, education is a key part of cultural capital along with family socialisation. We can now begin to see how parents' experiences of being parented influence how they parent. Additionally, their experiences of education can influence their expectations and aspirations for their children along with how they support them in their education. Subsequently, this impacts on their children's capitals. Capitals are developed throughout childhood and adulthood and exchanged in different fields, for example, employment. Employment is seen as a contributory factor of symbolic capital, which ascribes socially recognised and sanctioned prestige or honour, as discussed in Chapter 3.

You are now developing your understanding of how the accumulation of capitals (Bourdieu, 1977, 1984) determines an individual's exclusion or inclusion within society. Additionally, we can see how the notion of generational socialisation, for example, children exhibit the same traits and patterns of behaviour as their parents, becomes the norm. Here we can make reference to social learning theory (Parker and Ashencaen Crabtree, 2020; Walker and Horner, 2020). The families identified within the government policies are believed to be at risk, to themselves and others, because of their immoral, anti-social behaviour or intentional disengagement from education and employment. Discursive practices follow a blame-stigma pattern, in which the behaviour/lifestyle is first distanced from, followed by blame and subsequently these families being stigmatised. Media and social representations contribute towards the construction of social identities, which usually follow government representations. Let's reflect on the ladder on inference (Chapter 2), and revisit the questions where do we get our beliefs from, and where do we get our values from. We will now focus on a government policy, initially through a Research Summary, followed by exploring the potential implications of such a policy.

Research summary

Phase 1 (2012–2015) of the Troubled Families initiative defined troubled families living in households who:

- Are involved in crime and anti-social behaviour,
- Have children not in school or high levels of truancy,
- Have an adult on out-of-work benefits,
- Cause high costs to the public purse.

Phase 2 (2015–2020) expanded this definition to include that each family must have at least two of the following problems:

1. Parents or children involved in crime or anti-social behaviour,
2. Children who have not been attending school regularly,
3. Children who need help: children of all ages, who need help, are identified as in need or are subject to a Child Protection Plan,

(Continued)

4. Adults out of work or at risk of financial exclusion or young people at risk of worklessness,
5. Families affected by domestic violence and abuse,
6. Parents or children with a range of health problems.

(Loft, 2020)

Research undertaken by Wills et al. (2017) summarised the Troubled Families initiative by explaining that the aim of the programme was to save money. The programme was based on financial incentives and a payment by results scheme. Local authorities had to demonstrate a set of outcomes to receive funding. Interventions were provided by a lead worker with the aim of improving family outcomes. The Troubled Family initiative was identified as reminiscent to the 'social residuum' of the 1880s, the 'problem family' of the 1950s and 'cycle of deprivation of the 1970s' (Welshman, 2007, 2013) and the underclass discourse of the 1980s (Murray, 1990). However, a distinction needs to be made between families that have troubles, families that are troubled and those that cause trouble (Wills et al., 2017). In their research, Wills et al. (2017) identified three themes: getting into trouble, becoming troubled and being troublesome.

Getting into trouble included a loss of a supportive network, loss through death or separation, teenage motherhood, frequent house moves and domestic abuse.
Becoming troubled included lone parenthood, a negative sense of self from child-hood, or as a result of a life event, social isolation or abuse from neighbours. Partners were described as being a threat or being absent.
Being troublesome included experience of formal services. These services were described as either late with the support offered or interfering. Services became involved at a crisis point or child protection.

The authors (Wills et al., 2017) questioned the legitimacy of such labelling, 'troubled families', acknowledging that each family, in their research, had complex needs, a lack of support, experienced 'life events' and domestic abuse.

Comment

The Troubled Families initiative is an interesting example of how government policies are frequently portrayed as supportive and for the benefit of individuals, individuals who are represented as a risk to themselves and others, but disguise the undercurrent philosophy that these are not typical 'nuclear' families within a functionalist perspective as discussed earlier in this chapter. Therefore, it could be suggested that the Troubled Families initiative is simply a steer to gain control, regain traditionalism and 'fix' the problem of broken Britain (Crossley, 2018). However, and as discussed previously, the nuclear family was an idealisation and not the norm. There is also some similarity with the discourse of the Troubled Families initiative and that of teenage pregnancy, as discussed in Chapter 2, in that these individuals are a problem.

You can also see how representations and identity construction involve both a value and moral dimension, discussed in Chapter 2, along with symbolic power, discussed in

Chapter 3. Again, you could consider the ladder of inference, Chapter 2, and how beliefs can lead to assumptions and contribute towards the construction of knowledge. Additionally, we can also see how 'working-class people have been de-valued over time because of their class positions' (Mckenzie, 2018, p. 27). The question to be asked is, has the Troubled Families initiative labelled a group of families without giving consideration to their personal situation and circumstances.

The concept of 'troubled families' provides an example of the strength of official government discourse. 'Troubled families' have been given an official state identity. The government have identified how many 'troubled families' there are, and roughly where they can be found.

(Crossley, 2018, p. 60)

It is such discourse that Bourdieu (1991) refers to as symbolic power, as discussed in Chapter 3. The government is exercising their power, which carries a legitimacy, and as a consequence, families become labelled, identified and represented as such, for example, 'troubled families'.

The continuing marginalisation of issues of poverty, inequality and material deprivation in the 'troubled families' discourse helps to portray the issues faced by families as originating within the home, and also close off the opportunity to consider the influence of these structural factors on the lives of 'troubled families'.

(Crossley, 2018, p. 81)

We introduced the ecological framework (Bronfenbrenner, 1979/2005) in Chapter 3, and here you can observe how the macrosystem and structural factors have the potential to significantly impact upon the individual's microsystem. Additionally, you can observe how individual microsystems influence government policy. As a social worker, you need to have an understanding of such interactional systems, the potential of such initiatives to further marginalise families, but also the oppressiveness of such labels. Indeed, as we saw in Chapter 2, such labels lead towards stereotyping and inferiorisation. Such understanding contributes towards what a social worker should know, discussed in Chapter 1, and can be identified within the PCF, for example, Diversity and Equality and Rights, Justice and Economic Well-Being. It is part of our role, as social workers, to enable these families to tell their story, the journey to where they are today, what it is like living within their situation and circumstances. As a social worker, we need to prevent, protect and safeguard children from abuse, but we also need to empower families and advocate on their behalf to support change. We can only do this by effective communication, listening and working in partnership with them.

Case study

Lisa's partner died eight months ago. Lisa did not work, she looked after their three children. Her partner was employed and received the national minimum wage. This meant that they were unable to build up any savings. Lisa is on welfare benefits.

(Continued)

She would like to attend a local college to complete an access course and has aspirations to go to university and become a nurse. Lisa and her partner had discussed this and she was hoping to do so in future. However, with three young children, and little financial resources, she is unable to afford childcare and the college does not have the facilities. Lisa remains on welfare benefits and is unemployed.

Activity 4.9

Reflecting on the research summary, and considering the three themes identified getting into trouble, becoming troubled and being troublesome and the Case Study, which theme best describes Lisa's situation? Why?
How could she be supported in her desire to attend college and university?
What would be the long-term benefits if Lisa was to become a nurse?
For Lisa? The children? The family?

Invisible families

There are many individuals who are part of a family but for various reasons have become estranged, for example, unaccompanied asylum-seeking children and young people, refugees and homeless people. According to the Refugee Council, the United Kingdom received 2,291 applications for asylum from unaccompanied children in 2020. These children are separated from their family, many fleeing danger, some are trafficked and others bereaved. These children are vulnerable.

Unaccompanied asylum-seeking children

Unaccompanied asylum-seeking children are looked after by the local authority either in residential homes or with foster carers. These children are in another country, experiencing language barriers, cultural differences and living with the knowledge that they might never see their parents, siblings or wider family members again. Working with these children requires sensitivity and an awareness of their journey to where they are today. A journey that can be only told by the child themselves. Building trust and developing the relationship where you can explore that journey can be difficult because of previous experiences. Communication is essential and might include visual as well as verbal interactions (Koprowska, 2020). Working with interpreters is invaluable but this also comes with its own challenges of communication, interpreting and explaining what you are doing and why. Within your practice, you need to be aware that engaging children can also be very easy and this presents a risk. A risk because sometimes individuals engage, groom and promise children they can help, keep them safe and look after them. Gaining the trust is then, often, followed by exploitation and abuse.

Refugees

Refugees, similar to the children discussed above, are usually fleeing danger, some are trafficked and others bereaved. According to the 1951 United Nations Convention, a definition of the term 'refugee' refers to a person who fulfils the conditions of paragraph 2 of this section:

> *(2) ... owing to a well-founded fear of being persecuted for reasons of race, religion, nationality, membership of a particular social group or political opinion, is outside the country of his nationality and is unable or, owing to such fear, is unwilling to avail himself of the protection of that country; or who, not having a nationality and being outside the country of his former habitual residence as a result of such events, is unable or, owing to such fear, is unwilling to return to it.*
>
> (United Nations High Commissioner for Refugees, undated, p. 14)

There are many similarities between unaccompanied children and refugees; for example, many refugees are separated from their families and friends, experience language and cultural barriers and have a distrust of individuals because of their previous experiences. Their journey to where they are today is often fraught with difficulties and challenges. Refugees are frequently stereotyped, stigmatised and marginalised. Their legal status presents problems in relation to welfare benefits, employment and housing. Such structural problems prevent these individuals from starting a new life, exploring education and employment opportunities and having the safety and security of a home they can call their own.

As social workers we need to be aware of and have an understanding of the legalities, including the legal status, of unaccompanied asylum-seeking children and refugees while at the same time being sensitive to their needs, strengths and potential risks. These children, young people and adults are part of a family. A family they may never see again. Without stability, safety, security and employment, they are less likely to see. There are many structural factors associated with status and many of these we, as social workers, will not be able to change; however, we can challenge the injustice of stigmatisation and marginalisation. We can support these individuals, we can listen to them about their journey and their aspirations and we can advocate on their behalf.

Homeless

There are many homeless families: '135,000 children in Britain are homeless' and there are '5,683 homeless families with children currently living in emergency B&Bs and hostels' (Shelter, 2019).

These families are often invisible from the public gaze. They typically live in one room, which exacerbates their situation and circumstances. Their accommodation is often temporary, which frequently results in them being labelled as transient families. When they are unemployed, they are faced with difficult situations; for example, what address do they put on a job application form? These families typically find themselves in a downward spiral of welfare dependency, are unable to secure employment and are at risk of exploitation. Many are estranged from wider family members and friends.

Additionally, there are many single homeless people who are parents. Through relationship breakdown, separation or because of many other reasons, they have become estranged from their children. Some people have had their children removed and taken into care, while others, separated or divorced, have found themselves homeless resulting in the loss of contact with their children and their children not seeing them. Many of these homeless individuals have become disconnected from the world of family life, some through choice, others through situation and circumstances. Nevertheless, it is highly likely that their journey to where they are today included being once part of a family.

Individuals with a disability and who are also parents

Individuals with a disability and who are parents are often invisible and at the same time experience discrimination and stigmatisation. However, having a disability is only part of their identity as is being a parent. In the United Kingdom, about a fifth (21%) of two-parent households have a parent with a disability in comparison to single-parent households (27%) or about 1 in 4.

Being a single parent with a disability can present many challenges depending on their personal situation, circumstances and availability of support; many are said to feel isolated and overwhelmed. However, many issues begin prior to becoming a parent. Individuals with a disability who wish to become a parent frequently report derogatory comments and negative attitudes when expressing and seeking advice about becoming a parent and during pregnancy. There are often issues around attending appointments, communication difficulties and the birth itself. Research identified that health and social care professionals are not following government guidelines around family assessments and eligibility for support in relation to parents with a disability (Munro and Zonouzi, 2018). Parents with a disability have the same rights as parents without a disability. There is no legislation in relation to being an individual with a disability who is also a parent. However, there is legislation and guidance to protect the rights of individuals with disabilities. Many individuals with a disability, who are also parents, report that they are often invisible when support is needed, but highly visible with regards to their parenting ability. Their parenting ability is often questioned and challenged and they are frequently perceived to be placing their children at risk.

Activity 4.10

Observe the world around you; what do you see? Do you see individuals, children, young people, adults? Do you see families? Revisit Activity 4.1, Activity 4.2, Activity 4.3 and Activity 4.5 and reconsider your answers; this time thinking about the visibility, representation and meaning of 'family'.

Comment

Families are represented in many different ways; for example, families are represented in government documents, as discussed previously, families are also represented within the media and social media; however, are all families represented? Are all individuals included? As we can see, there are individuals and families who are clearly invisible within the 'family discourse', 'typical family' representations and support needs, but yet they are clearly visible within the labelling, categorisation and questioning of their parenting ability. This frequently leads to marginalisation and stigmatisation. Therefore, when working with children, young people, adults and families, we need to build trust, we need to learn about their experiences and their journey and we need to listen to what they are saying and gain an understanding of their world. Once again, we see the importance of communication skills.

Research summary

Research undertaken by Walsh and Mason (2018) examines family diversity including single-parent, cohabitating, same-sex and transnational families in relation to social work practice. The research illustrates the importance of the need for social workers to be aware of family structures and practices. They identified that:

- Social workers focus on the mother and less on the father. Males are often seen as a threat to the children, mother or social worker.
- Social workers need to develop their knowledge and skills in relation to working with migrant families. Social workers need to be aware of cultural sensitivities, which are often undermined by organisational and system constraints, for example, deadlines and timescales. Such constraints have implications for decision-making.
- Social workers stereotypically identify gendered caring roles in the family.
- The institutional embeddedness of normative gendered assumptions, for example, mothers as main carers and excluding fathers. Although the legal status of parental responsibility does play an influential part in whether to include or not the father irrespective of the relationship between the male and the children.
- Working with migrant families where there is complexity with associated living conditions, housing and especially multiple occupancy, employment, childcare, abuse, employee issues, problems and difficulties.

Comment

There are also systemic constraints for both families and social workers where time and resources are limited. Social workers need to recognise contemporary families as being diverse and multifaceted. There is a disconnect between UK-based norms and expectations of families, the promotion of gender inequality and acceptance of traditional gendered practice within families and contemporary family life. There is also a personal disconnect for many individuals, for example, unaccompanied asylum seekers, refugees and the homeless. Further, there are multiple factors that are intertwined and need to be considered in relation to social work interventions and the decision-making process. Here you could revisit the ladder of inference, Chapter 2, and reconsider your own values, beliefs and assumptions in addition to cultural humility, Table 2.2, Chapter 2, and reflect on how you see yourself working with children and families.

Activity 4.11

Over a one-week period, look at a range of magazines, commercial advertisements such as billboard posters, posters on buses, trams and other commercial vehicles, on the internet and on television programmes and advertisements, for examples of how families are represented.
Create a reflective account about family representations noting family composition, for example, the number of adults and children and also the gender of the parents and children. Observe ethnicity, disability and how families are constructed and portrayed. What are your observations?

Comment

What are your observations from this Activity? How are families represented in the media? Did you note any similarities or differences? Through your observations, were these representations typical of families and family life within your community and how you defined a family in Activity 4.2?

Describing family life

Thinking about family and what family means brings us to another question; how do we describe family life? Those everyday occurrences, the comings and goings, the mundane and the excitement of daily family life. Here we could consider the concept of 'family practices' (Morgan, 1996). Within this concept, Morgan (1996, 2011, 2013) refers to the everyday nuances, the structures and routines of daily life – those aspects that make up everyday living within a family.

Activity 4.12

Consider a typical day in your life. Write down a day in the life of ... (you). Focus your writing on family life, who do you include in your family, what do you do – individually and together, what makes up a typical day. Within your writing include those structures, routines and aspects that contribute towards your family practices.

Morgan (2011) acknowledges that there are differing explanations in relation to describing family life, but concludes that the term 'family practices' is relevant in that it emphasises that families 'do' (p. 11) things rather than refer to 'the' (p. 11) family. The significance of 'doing' clearly indicates that families do things together. For example, sitting at the table eating a meal. When thinking about this typical activity, there are many different stages that may be considered such as do we eat the meal with some, but not all family members, or together as a family. We could consider a wide variety of activities which contribute towards family practices or enable family practice to be undertaken. For example, an individual could shop and purchase food. Two or more family members might prepare and cook the food, which enables the family to enjoy the meal. Through all these elements there is the notion of 'doing' – family participation that includes various experiences that culminate in a meal. However, this same example could be retold in many different ways. Again, this demonstrates the complexity and differences of what we mean by family, who do we include and how family practices are played out.

Activity 4.13

Consider the above example and think how you would retell the scenario for your family. Who would do the shopping, the preparing, the cooking of the food? Do you sit down together at the table? Do you share experiences and discuss your day? Or watch television? What are your family practices?

Comment

This activity encourages you to start thinking about how family practices may be experienced. You may have highlighted the importance of sharing and contributing to the making of the meal, which in turn may contribute to family experiences. Within this we need to recognise that for each family the circumstances are unique and will have a personal narrative attached. This demonstrates the need for us, as social workers, to always be aware that the notion of family is complex and that families are not a homogenous group. Each family, retelling this scenario, would give different meanings and importance to each part of the story. Let's consider those invisible families discussed previously, consider how 'doing family' could be different. Those everyday experiences might be different and for many, how 'their' family may not include biological family members, but instead other individuals they have met because of their situation and circumstances. How would they retell the scenario? Here we can observe how individuals are part of a family, but not always a part of a family, while others are visible by the assumptions that are made about their family.

Within the concept of family practices, the everyday nuances, structures and routines are not necessarily conducted within the home environment, but could be during activities, outings and include extended family members. Again, who do we refer to, and include, when we talk about family and in particular 'our family'. Additionally, there is an interplay between family members and an interconnectedness between culture and structural factors. Bringing the concept of family practices to the world of today and the proliferation of digital technology, family practices could be considerably different from when Morgan first conceived the idea in 1996. Exploring the notion of family practices from the perspective of the digital world would now incorporate a vast range of social media which enables families to remain in contact and visually see each other, partic ipate in celebrations and play together through technology. Therefore, family practices now include those nuances, structures and routines that could also incorporate 'doing' digital family practices. Does this add to family experiences, the sense of belonging and meaning of family? Does technology enable us to connect and interreact; 'I have arrived at the supermarket'; 'while at the supermarket, please could you get …'; 'I have arrived at school'. Today, technology is as much a part of family practices as the individuals who are a part of the family.

Displaying families

Building on the concept of family practices, along with how technology has changed everyday life including communication and presentation, we could also consider how we 'display' being a family (Finch, 2007). Finch describes how families want to be seen as a family. This raises the question of whether this is social conditioning, a part of our socialisation or conformity to the notion of the nuclear family? Individuals perceive the need to both feel that they are a family and 'display' to the world that they are a family. What was once a family ritual of 'bringing out the photo album' and the showing of photographs has been replaced with passing around the mobile device. They are displaying an array of photographs depicting celebrations, outings, activities and all displaying family life to family and friends and to some extent the world. The photo album has been replaced by the 'cloud', the storage place of photographs which is accessible from a variety of digital devices and from across the world. The notion of displaying family and wanting to be seen as a family also provides reassurance that they belong to and are a family, although not always subscribing to the 'traditional' family norms and therefore with the potential of placing their visibility, of non-traditionality, to the fore. Returning to Activity 4.11 and your observations and reflections of family representations, how are families represented? Are families displayed as the 'traditional' nuclear family? Or displayed to represent the diversity of family formations today?

Activity 4.14

Considering the notion of displaying families, think about a family you know, how do they display themselves as a family?

Chapter summary

This chapter began by exploring what we mean by 'family', the conceptualisation of the nuclear family and asked whether this was the predominant family structure. Contemporary family formations were explored including asking whether a person living alone is a family or an individual with their relationships with other individuals being online. This returns us to the question what is meant by family, in addition to recognising the diversity of family formations. Social workers need to understand how the macrosystem, the social, economic and political, impacts individuals and families and we began to explore this through highlighting some of the government initiatives. You looked at the significance of the language and labelling and how these initiatives might be oppressive. We introduced the concept of invisible families and how some individuals and families were part of a family, but often due to no fault of their own had become estranged. Through structural factors they become invisible, excluded and marginalised, but at the same time are visible and stigmatised. In the final section of the chapter, you started to consider how family life is described and displayed. In the next chapter, we will focus our attention on working with children and young people.

Further reading

Dobson, J and Melrose, A (eds) (2021) *Working with Children, Families and Young People Professional Dilemmas, Perspectives and Solutions*. Oxon: Routledge.

This book provides an introduction to working with children, young people and families. This is not a social work text but details important aspects of working with children and families. The book explores the children's workforce, self-development and building confidence. Additionally, there is an overview of working with marginalisation and empowerment. The book explores people's lived experiences including exploring family vulnerabilities, poverty and policy landscapes.

Parker, J and Ashencaen Crabtree, S (2018) *Social Work with Disadvantaged and Marginalised People*. London: Sage/Learning Matters.

This book focuses on developing knowledge and understanding of disadvantage and marginalisation and the impact on people lives. The book introduces complex concepts of disadvantage and marginalisation. It examines the knowledge and skills needed to work with individuals experiencing disadvantage and marginalisation and explores practising ethically and reflexively. The book examines communities on the margins, labelling and deviance and how such aspects need to be considered within social work practice.

5

Working with children

> (Continued)
>
> It will also introduce you to the following standards as set out in the Social Work Subject Benchmark Statement (2019):
>
> **5.4**   Service users and carers
> **5.15** Communication skills
> **5.16** Skills in working with others
>
> *See Appendix 2 for a detailed description of these standards.*

Introduction

In this chapter, we will focus on working with children and young people. We will begin with a brief reference to Chapter 2, and the functionalist perspective of the nuclear family and the socialisation of children. The socialisation of children remains, for example the home environment, school and community; however, the landscape of childhood has changed and we will briefly look at some of these changes. The coronavirus pandemic (COVID-19) has had a significant impact on everybody's lives including children and young people. Within our discussion on COVID-19 we will explore children's engagement with family, friends, education and the absence of socialisation. The chapter will then explore the mental well-being of children and some of the reasons why the levels of anxiety and depression, among children and young people are increasing. Here we will pay particular attention to bullying and intimate personal violence. The final section of the chapter will make reference to the dramaturgical approach to reflection discussed in Chapter 1. However, rather than reflecting on the work undertaken, we will use this model to reflect on how we might work with children and young people.

Childhood, children and young people

As you journey through the social work degree, you will encounter many discussions in relation to childhood, children and young people. You will observe how the historical landscape of childhood has changed significantly. You will discover the social construction of childhood, the wider political and cultural constructions and the importance of intergenerational relationships. In Chapter 4, we explored the functionalist perspective and the nuclear family. As we explored, we discovered that Parsons observed society as being a functioning organism where a significant element was the family – the parents and home environment. Here we can recognise Bronfenbrenner's (1979/2005) ecology of human development, explored in Chapter 3, and the relationship between parents, children and the home environment. It was in the home environment where children were predominantly socialised to become the next workforce, parents and ensure social equilibrium. The conceptual tools of Bourdieu (1977, 1984, 1991), as discussed in Chapter 3, are evident here, for instance habitus; the socialisation of the children to the societal norms and expectations, developing their capitals; preparing for the next workforce, and field; maintaining the status quo. Thus, importance was placed on the family to provide, and ensure, that children became appropriate adults.

The changing landscape of childhood

Childhood, in the UK, has changed significantly since the 1950s, children are now seen as social actors, having agency, and being members of society. Children's rights, for example their and engagement participation in decision-making about their lives has become embedded within the culture of society. National policy and legal changes, within the UK, included the Children Act 1989, which introduced the principles of seeing the child as an individual, children having a right to be legally represented, and having a right to be consulted about decisions which directly affect them. We can see the results of these changes and how having agency has given children rights, a voice and say in relation to their lives and the care they receive. Nevertheless, there is a need for adults to support, protect and advocate on behalf of children. Indeed, this should include listening to children, for example the words and language they use and non-verbal communication together with facial expressions and body language. However, despite the many changes, there continues to be concerns such as poverty, abuse and the welfare of children particularly with their mental well-being. It is estimated that in 2019–2020 there were 4.3 million children living in poverty in the UK, which equates to 31 per cent of children, or nine children in a classroom of 30 (Child Poverty Action Group, 2021). Furthermore in 2019, 49,570 children in England and 4,810 children in Wales were looked after by their local authority because of their experiences or risk of abuse or neglect (Office for National Statistics, 2020).

Activity 5.1

Thinking about how childhood has changed over the last 20 years, what do you feel are the most significant changes?

The coronavirus pandemic (COVID-19)

Socialisation, as we have identified previously, is an important aspect of child development. For many children this includes the home environment where family and friends visit, going to school, belonging to a club or engaging in activities. However, during COVID-19, there were restrictions of movement for many individuals. This included lockdowns which limited travel opportunities, changes in working patterns and some people being required to shield (not going out at all). During the pandemic, children, except in specific circumstances, did not attend school. The majority received homeschooling, and along with restricted movements, the socialisation aspect of schooling, extracurricular activities, hobbies and other activities ceased. Further, the socialisation aspect of family life and seeing friends was severely disrupted. Grandparents, aunts, uncles and cousins, along with friends, were unable to visit and offer their support. With such an important aspect of childhood missing what impact in the short and long term will this have on children?

Technology has facilitated the opportunity for some children to continue to have contact with wider family members; however, many grandparents are significant carers and they have not been able to engage in these roles online. Many children maintained their friendships through the internet, but this is not the same as face-to-face interactions. Additionally, such interactions are not just with other children, but also with adults whether they are family members, teachers or other adults within their lives. Building capital (Bourdieu, 1977, 1984) online is different from building it when face-to-face. During face-to-face interactions, confidence, self-esteem and communication skills, both verbal and non-verbal are developed, whereas online this is limited. In addition, etiquette along with unwritten rules, games of play and terms of reference are also identified and developed which contribute to a child's learning about becoming a social being in different environments. Outdoor play is an important contributory factor for child development; however, this was potentially limited during the pandemic. Many children have a garden to play in, possibly with siblings, but what about those who live in flats, tower blocks, or do not have access to a garden? Or as noted in the previous chapter, bed and breakfast establishments or hostels? Some families are living in one room. For these children, opportunities for outdoor activities during the pandemic were severely restricted. When we start to critically think about this, the potential impact is huge.

Activity 5.2

Thinking about the children you know, what are your observations of children socialising with other children, extended family members, friends? Did you notice any changes, during COVID-19, in children's

* behaviour,
* communication,
* confidence,
* motivation.

Parents working at home

The unprecedented situation during the pandemic meant that many aspects of family life changed. This included the home environment where children and parents were working or learning online. The home became the office, but yet it continued to be the family home for the children. For older children, there may have been some under-standing about these changes, but what about very young children? How does a parent explain to their two-year-old that they have to make a telephone call or attend a meeting? Two parent families might have had the advantage of managing this situation through sharing the childcare and arranging appointments at different times, but this might not always have been realistic and possible. What about single parents? Who cared for the children? Again, we can see the potential impact of the pandemic, although we will not know the true impact for many years. Here we can make reference to Bronfenbrenner's (1979/2005) ecological framework and Bourdieu's (1977, 1984) habitus and capital whereby a child's development is dependent upon actions and interactions, intersecting between environments, and within wider political, economic and social milieus. The time element within the PPCT (Bronfenbrenner, 2005) is also important. Children have had limited opportunities to spend time with extended family and friends during the pandemic, also they have not had time in the school environment or been able to engage in social activities and, importantly having time alone. Time alone is good, but we need to differentiate between time alone and isolation. Time is needed for children to move from dependency and develop their independence and thus enable them to create their own identity.

Research summary

Child abuse

- During the pandemic, child abuse increased.
- Child abuse referrals would normally come from a variety of sources including health visitors and schools, however, with school closures and health visitors being either redeployed or undertaking online visits the number of referrals declined.
- Some incidents of child abuse became invisible as social workers worked online, had reduced visits or met families, where possible, in their gardens.
- For children who were already experiencing abuse or neglect by household members, confinement at home meant prolonged exposure to potential harm.
- Lockdown meant fewer opportunities for children to be seen, supported or protected.
- Lockdown also increased some children's exposure to people who could harm them online.

Well-being

- Some health visitors were redeployed to assist with COVID-19 meaning that many new mothers and babies did not receive their support or services. Additionally, when health visitors provided support, this was often online.
- Children have said that family tensions and financial concerns, as well as feeling isolated from friends and fear about COVID-19, caused distress.
- One in four young people felt unable to cope with life following the start of the pandemic. This increased to 40 per cent among those are NEET.

(Continued)

(Continued)

- Children with a disability received reduced specialist health care, support and education. Many children remained at home with no out of home social contact, respite or external stimulation. This also placed additional stress on families.
- COVID-19 negatively affected the health and well-being of children with special educational needs and disabilities (SEND), in particular, their behaviour, emotions and mental health.
- Many young people who are supported through mental health services were unable to access support. Additionally, many support mechanisms such as friends and family, physical activity or being outdoors was not possible.
- One in eight children aged 5–19 in England has a diagnosable mental health condition. COVID-19 resulted in heightened feelings of anxiety and low-mood and other mental health conditions.

Education

- The closure of schools had a significant impact on children and young people. Besides education, schools are also places where children socialise, develop emotionally and, for some, find protection.
- With school closures, children and young people were homeschooled, but many received no education at all.
- Being homeschooled presented problems for many children and families. The digital divide, and disparities in support, between more affluent and less affluent households meant that many children could not access the internet. This made homeschooling and education almost impossible. Additionally, the forced closure of public libraries and those within schools had detrimental consequences meaning children could not access their facilities. With increased financial constraints placed on low-income families, they were less likely to be in a position to be able to buy computer equipment, books or other resources for their children.
- Refugee and asylum-seeking children who had already experienced a disrupted education through displacement also struggled to continue their education.

Parents/families

- During the pandemic, there was a significant increase in domestic abuse. There was also a reduction in support services and thus a decrease in the opportunities for women to leave abusive relationships.
- The pandemic placed increased stress on many families, including rising levels of unemployment and subsequent financial insecurity.
- The £1,000 uplift in the Universal Credit (UC) standard allowance provided around £20 per week extra support for working and non-working families. However, the time delay, a typical five-week wait for payments, when applying for UC when individuals become unemployed placed additional stress on families many of whom experienced financial difficulties.
- Women in lower socio-economic positions were more likely than women in higher socio-economic positions and men in general to be furloughed.

(Continued)

- COVID-19 placed even greater pressure on workers in groups already at higher risk of poverty including low-pay sectors, minority ethnic groups and lone parents.
- Furlough, reductions in working hours along with applying for UC caused even greater uncertainty around finances.
- Thirty-two per cent of private-renting employees and 34% of social-renting employees were furloughed by their employers. This placed additional stress on families.
- Many parents and carers faced financial insecurity, alterations to their routine, and the juggling of multiple responsibilities including work, full-time childcare and care for family members who were shielding or ill.

(See further reading, at the end of this chapter, for COVID-19 sources of information.)

The above is an overview of the impact COVID-19 has had on children, parents and families. Furlough was suggested by the government to assist the economy by limiting the number of redundancies that occurred as a result of the COVID-19 pandemic. Organisations that were unable to maintain their workforce were encouraged to furlough employees rather than make redundancies and apply for the Coronavirus Job Retention Scheme, which reimbursed employers with 80% of workers' wages.

Activity 5.3

What do you think will be the biggest impact of COVID-19 on children?

Comment

The pandemic has disrupted all aspects of life. Equally, the way we work with children and engage with families has also changed with much of this work being undertaken online and limited face-to-face work. We can see that children may have been placed at greater risk of abuse, become isolated and experienced significant disruption in their education and thus the enormity of such is yet to be fully identified. It could be argued that the pandemic will have a significant impact on children's lives potentially throughout their lifetime. This will include their development and education but also psychologically and socially. Here we can identify the PCF domains–Knowledge, Context and Organisations and Professional Leadership.

Evolving childhood

We can infer, so far from this chapter, that childhood is not a static phenomenon but rather a fluid and everchanging occurrence. Such changes are from within the family home: microsystem (Bronfenbrenner, 1979/2005), along with societal, economic and political: macrosystem (Bronfenbrenner, 1979/2005). Changes are also at a community and local level, in addition to national and international levels. Simultaneously, children's growth and development continue. Generally, child development is understood through developmental psychology, for example, cognitive, emotional and social processes (Parker and Ashencaen Crabtree, 2020; Walker and Horner, 2020). More recently there has been significant research into epigenetics and neuroscience (Wastell and White, 2017) and how these two areas contribute towards child development.

Walker and Horner (2020) observe that as children develop, they learn emotional and social skills that support their understanding of relationships with family and friends: 'as a social worker you will need to gain an understanding of the 'whole' child, their development and their life course' (Walker and Horner, 2020, p. 56). The whole person perspective would also include spirituality 'a closer analysis of our human evolution reveals that every human being can be constructed as a composite "whole" holistic being; comprised of physical, psychological, social and spiritual dimensions' (McSherry et al., 2020, p. 107).

Ecological framework

In Chapter 3, we explored how Bronfenbrenner's (1979/2005) ecological framework incorporates all of these aspects of human growth and development. This includes the interconnecting systems of the family, community and society where interactions and actions impact upon, directly and indirectly, the child's microsystem. Such interconnectivity has the potential to impact the child's health and well-being, their mental health and their cognitive ability not just through childhood but across their lifespan. The chronosystem enables the impact of life events and experiences to be identified on subsequent development (Bronfenbrenner, 2005). Giving children agency, rights and ensuring that their voice is heard has been hugely significant; however, at the same time there are enormous pressures placed on children, for example educational attainment, body image, the wearing of the 'right' clothes and having the latest technological gadgets. These are contributory factors to healthy, or unhealthy, growth and development, mental well-being and a sense of belonging.

Habitus and capitals

As discussed in Chapter 3, habitus and capital (Bourdieu, 1977, 1984) are significant aspects that are developed throughout childhood and adulthood. A significant part of socialisation is the way the child develops. Initially, this will be through the immediate family including parents and siblings, extending to wider family members, friends and the community. The child's habitus is developed through this socialisation as they grow into a social being and develop their unique self. Contributory factors of this unique self will include being listened to and being seen, recognised and acknowledged in their own right, in addition to life events and experiences all of which will develop self-confidence and authenticity. It is these aspects that contribute towards the child's habitus, their predispositions and characteristics. However, the impact of the pressures noted above are also contributory factors. Therefore, we can see how the child's habitus can be influenced by a multiplicity of factors. Additionally, as the child is socialised within their immediate world of family and friends they are developing and building their capitals. This continues to develop as they start school, expand their network of friends, community activities and broaden their experiences. The interconnectedness of habitus and the development of capitals is intrinsic, for example if the child experiences bullying, this could impact on their self-confidence. This could result in them withdrawing, impacting further on their self-confidence along with their mental well-being and reducing their social interactions. Thus, the likelihood of the child developing their capitals is reduced. Additionally, this could impact on their education, which has the potential to add further pressure and the downward spiral continues and affects their health and well-being and subsequent engagement in their various fields (Bourdieu, 1984, 1991).

Working with children and young people

The significance of the family home, along with family history and functioning, cannot be underestimated with regards to child development. Additionally, we need to remember that there are wider influences too, from extended family members and friends. The community is also a significant contributory factor. You can gain a greater understanding of the child's life when you explore the interconnectivity of these different interacting systems that are a part of, and impact on, the child's microsystem. When you explore the child's developing habitus, you can begin to see how internal and external factors can have a positive and negative impact. How those different impacts are managed are crucial and therefore, when working with children you need to be supporting the development of their problem-solving skills, encouraging and empowering them to adopt a strengths-based approach along with a solution-focused approach. These approaches require working in partnership with children, good communication skills including listening attentively and encouraging the child to take the lead. Your role is to support and empower the child to talk and create their own plan. These approaches can also be adopted when working with parents or with children and parents together. Here we can make links to the PCF domains – Knowledge, Skills and Interventions and Professionalism. However, because of the relationship between all of the PCF domains, as discussed in Chapter 1, we can see the significance of the other domains, such as Values and Ethics or Diversity and Equality.

Problem-solving

A problem-solving approach is based on a task-centred approach (Teater, 2020). You support the child in the identification of the problem, or what they would like to change, and together you break this down to a series of tasks. The tasks need to be achievable and within an agreed timescale. It is much better to have a number of tasks that are achievable than one task that might be overwhelming. Each task is incremental and therefore builds on the previous one to achieve the desired goal.

Strengths-based approach

A strengths-based approach (Kondrat, 2020; Saleeby, 2009; Witkin, 2017) focuses on the child's strengths. You help and support the child to discover and develop their strengths. Through explorative discussion with the child, you identify what they are good at, a strength (strengths), and develop this strength (strengths) to solve their problem or make changes. For example, you could prompt the child by saying that you have observed that one of their strengths is how they are able to talk to you about how they are feeling. The focus is on what the child sees and feels as being a problem, not what you think the problem is. To develop their strengths, a task-centred approach could be applied.

Solution-focused approach

A solution-focused approach (Kondrat, 2020) focuses on communication to discover solutions to problems. This approach is very much about engaging with the child to work through the problem, or what they would like to change, and explore how the problem might be solved or how what they want to change might be accomplished. Once they have identified solutions, a task-centred approach could be applied along with a strengths-based approach to identify solutions in the future.

Developing skills

Working with children to develop the skills of problem-solving, adopting a strengths-based approach and identification of solutions is, firstly, recognising that these three approaches are applied by social workers in everyday practice. Secondly, as you become familiar with them, you come to role model them and facilitate the child's learning, development and application in their everyday lives. All three approaches require good communication skills, planning and development of open questions. This is not about you solving their problems or identifying solutions, but rather through explorative dialogue the child identifies what they feel is a problem, what their strengths are and the solution to that problem. Problems might sound quite negative; it may not be a problem but something they would like to change. Through questioning you identify the problem, or what they would like to change. The child describes the problem and through your questioning, together, you identify their strengths and solutions. Let's work through this with a case study and an activity.

Case study

Reena, aged 12, is becoming withdrawn, taking time away from school and getting distressed if her parents say she has to go out. Reena's parents say this is unusual because she normally enjoys going to school and has lots of friends.

Activity 5.4

Consider the different approaches outlined earlier. How are you going to find out what is happening in Reena's life? What questions do you need to ask?

Comment

There are potentially many reasons why Reena is not wanting to go to school. Did you consider that it could be because of bullying or transitioning from junior school to a new academy or a problem at home?

A **problem-solving approach** could be used to identify why Reena is not wanting to attend school. You could consider exploring Reena's microsystem and identify the individuals who are impacting on her microsystem. This will include her parents, wider family and friends, but could also be individuals at school.

A **strengths-based approach**: Did you note that Reena's parents said that she enjoyed school and had lots of friends? This could be explored by asking Reena what her favourite lessons are, what she likes about school, and encouraging her to talk about her friends. Something for you to think about is why she has lots of friends. Consider if she is kind, supportive, a good listener, exciting to be with, fun. Are these strengths? You could consider Reena's habitus, for example her characteristics such as identity, sense of belonging and confidence. Her parents have said that this is unusual for Reena and therefore ask yourself what might have changed. Reena has lots of friends, she is developing her social network, her capital (Bourdieu, 1984). Ask yourself what is impacting on this development. During your discussion, you observe that Reena has changed school, most of her friends are attending another school and she is being bullied.

A **solution-focused approach** might include exploring how she made friends previously. Reena talked to you about how her friends say that she is supportive, kind and fun. Could she make new friends at her new school? Could she continue to see her old friends after school or at the weekend? Could they interact on social media? You also identified that Reena was confident and was comfortable talking to people. You explore the bullying, and together talk about the importance of Reena talking to her parents. You could offer to talk to them together. You talk about the importance of school and telling them about the bullying and offer to arrange a meeting to discuss.

During these discussions, you are encouraging Reena to talk about and share her feelings and experiences, in addition to identifying the problems and how they could be solved. She is developing her confidence through the identification of strengths and what she is good at and arriving at her own solutions. Together you discuss timescales and create a plan.

Mental well-being

The mental well-being of children is increasingly a concern. Mental ill health among children has seen a significant rise between 1995 and 2014 (Pitchforth et al., 2019). Between 2017 and 2020, there has been a further rise:

Rates of probable mental disorders have increased since 2017. In 2020, one in six (16.0%) children aged 5 to 16 years were identified as having a probable mental disorder, increasing from one in nine (10.8%) in 2017. The increase was evident in both boys and girls.

(Vizard et al., 2020, p. 9)

There is a correlation between the increase in numbers for 2020 and the Coronavirus pandemic that we talked about above.

Public Health England describe mental well-being as:

more than the absence of mental illness and is inextricably linked with an individual's emotional, physical and social wellbeing. It is influenced by their resilience and physical health, relationships and the wider social, economic, cultural and environmental conditions in which they live.

(Bryant et al., 2015, p. 6)

Within the UK the rates of anxiety and depression, among children, are increasing. The main issues identified are stress, family or peer conflict, bullying and loss.

Children, young people and bullying

Bullying is widely recognised to be a significant problem affecting the health and well-being of children. Bullying is usually focused around a number of areas. These include:

- looking different, appearing to be different; this might include how they dress, or their physical appearance, or who they are friends with and socialise with,
- disability,
- the way a child presents themselves, behaves, acts,
- the age, class, gender, sexuality, ethnicity of the child,
- being a young carer,
- being bereaved of a parent or significant person,
- the area where they live, parent's employment, poverty.

Cyberbullying

Cyberbullying has become an increasing social issue with the rapid developments in technology and social media websites. This has resulted in many children experiencing online bullying. Cyberbullying is any form of bullying which takes place online. The significant difference between 'traditional bullying' and 'cyberbullying' is that the internet is available 24 hours a day. Therefore, cyberbullying can occur 24 hours a day, 7 days a week. It can be relentless and one child can be bullied by many others during the day, night and at the weekend. The potential for a wider audience means that a post online can be shared, manipulated and cannot be removed this can have devastating consequences.

The potential impact of bullying

Bullying can be devastating not just during childhood, but also into adulthood. There have been instances where children who have been bullied have self-harmed and some have committed suicide. Many children who are bullied experience mental ill health including depression and anxiety, have fewer friendships and experience isolation. School becomes a problem, which often leads to truancy or symptoms of ill health to avoid attendance.

Intimate partner violence

Intimate partner violence (IPV) is where two young people are in a relationship and one is experiencing physical, sexual or psychological abuse from their partner. This includes physical violence, coercion to engage in sexual activity, threats, ridicule or isolation. These do not occur in isolation, but are often interrelated and frequently lead to anxiety, depression and other health-related illnesses. Violence within teenage intimate relationships is increasing; additionally, there is a high level of emotional, physical and sexual violence between girls and their older partners (Barter et al., 2009; Fox et al., 2014). Kulkarni (2007) refers to the romance narrative and feminine ideals and the importance placed by the young women on maintaining the relationship even if it is abusive. This resonates with the historical associations, discussed in Chapter 4, in relation to the social norms and expectations of women (Abrams, 2002; Fink, 2011).

Working with children and young people

Within social work you will work with children experiencing many different aspects of life including:

- abuse and neglect,
- being looked after by foster carers or in children's homes,
- experiencing bullying, or relationship abuse during adolescence,
- criminally or sexually exploited,
- unaccompanied asylum seekers, refugees and homeless,
- from culturally diverse backgrounds,
- who identify as LGBT+,
- disability,
- caring for siblings, while others care for their parents and some are living with a parent with a life-limiting illness.

Besides the day-to-day lives of these children, many are experiencing abuse and neglect, marginalisation, stigmatisation and discrimination. As discussed in Chapter 1, when working with children, you need a wide range of knowledge and skills, the ability to reflect, solve problems and be able to think critically.

The dramaturgical approach to reflection

The dramaturgical approach to reflection was discussed in Chapter 1 in relation to reflecting on practice. The approach facilitates reflection through seven scenarios: the script, language, characters/actors, roles, venue, audience and editing process.

Activity 5.5

Revisit Chapter 1 and re-read the seven scenarios of the dramaturgical approach to reflection and work through the activities below.

Using reflection to plan and preparing for practice

In social work we often reflect on the work we have undertaken, rather than use reflection to think about our work retrospectively, we shall now look at how we can use this model to plan and prepare for working with children. This does not mean that we do not work in partnership with children. There should always be an emphasis on working together when planning any piece of work; nevertheless, we can reflect on what the purpose of our involvement is, what our intervention is, and what we need to consider along with asking ourselves some 'what if' questions. Here we will explore the seven scenarios of the dramaturgical approach to reflection with the focus on working with children. While working through these scenario's, think about the PCF domains, professional standards along with Figure 1.5 and Figure 2.2 Preparation for practice.

The script – placing the event, situation, circumstance into context. Consider here what the purpose of your involvement is; the reason why you are involved. You need to place importance on the child's voice, listening to what they have to say and in their own words. Communication skills are essential. Asking questions to find out about them can help build relationships. Many children do not trust people in authority and therefore developing trust is important. Some children will talk and tell you everything. Sometimes it is difficult to 'keep up' as they talk about one thing, quickly move on to something else and then return to the previous topic; you don't want to stop them because they might not wish to continue and you have lost the moment. Here you need to make a mental note of what they said and when they have finished talking, refer back and ask them to tell you more, or help you to understand (Davies and Duckett, 2019). You might work with children who don't want to speak at all, while others will avoid talking about anything relating to their current situation. Some children will talk about anything and everything and suddenly ask you a question or tell you something that you need to record (Davies and Duckett, 2019). In these circumstances it is important that you make sure this is recorded using the child's words. Within these circumstances you may need to act immediately, for example if a child is at risk of significant harm. This will be explored in the next chapter.

Things to consider

Things to consider when planning the work are time – chromosystem (Bronfenbrenner – Chapter 3): over what timescale, who was there/involved, who was not there/involved, tell me about…. Think about the 'field' (Bourdieu (1991) – Chapter 3) – the environment, the location where the event, situation or circumstance took place along with the hierarchal position of those involved. Here you are building a picture through the eyes of the child, of the event, situation, circumstance.

Activity 5.6

Think about the following questions and make a note of your answers.

- When meeting a child for the first time how would you introduce yourself?
- How would you introduce yourself if the child was non-verbal?
- How would you introduce yourself if the child did not speak English?
- Thinking about the previous questions, how would you ask the child to tell you about themselves?

The language – when working with children we need to be mindful of how we talk to them and the language, for example the words, we use. We need to avoid jargon, acronyms, colloquialisms and euphemisms. We need to explain clearly, in age, developmentally and cognitively appropriate language, why we are talking to them, what we will do with the information they tell us, who we will we share that information with, and what will happen next. This is significant in building trust with the child. Language is a key part of communication. We need to consider language in its simplest form, not over complicate it, but at the same time not be patronising. We need to be clear, ask one question at a time and consider the use of words and be prepared to explain the meaning to add clarity. We need to give children time to think about their answers and be aware that we may need to repeat questions to help them to process what is being asked.

Things to consider

Wherever possible ask open questions that will enable the child to talk, to explain, describe and not give one-word answers. Listen attentively, what are they saying, what words are they using and what are they not saying? Within all communication we need to observe their body language, is it congruent with what they are saying? For example, they may tell you that they are happy at home; however, you observe that they have their arms folded close against their body, they are looking down and their voice is quiet and unanimated.

The characters/actors – who's involved, who are the key players within the event, situation, circumstance. Consider the relationship between the child and their relationship with the other individuals involved. This could be their parents, wider family members or friends. The other individuals involved might not be connected to the family, but rather attend the same school, live within the community or belong to another community. They might be known to the child or not known. Other individuals might be professionals such as teachers or health professionals.

Things to consider

Consider the process-person-context-time (PPCT) model (Bronfenbrenner, 2005), for example the child's developmental stage, their cognitive ability, their interrelated systems and time. This should also include disability, ethnicity and sexual orientation.

Case study

Charlie, aged 14, is telling their parents that they do not feel well, they cannot go to school, and when they do go, they are leaving early or missing some lessons. They have stopped meeting with friends and appear anxious to use their mobile phone.

Activity 5.8

You want to know more about what is happening with Charlie. Consider the following questions:

- Who do you talk to?
- What questions do you ask Charlie?
- Do these questions change if Charlie is male or female?
- Do these questions take into consideration cultural diversity?

The roles – within any given event, situation, circumstance, there are characters and actors who are involved. Some of these will have a specific role, for example a parent, a teacher, and these will have responsibilities towards the child. Other individuals will not have roles or responsibilities towards the child. It is the social worker's responsibility to identify all individuals who are involved in any given event, situation, circumstance and the part they play. Again, we see the importance of the child's voice, the essential requirement of communication skills and the ability to engage the child in conversation.

Things to consider

When considering the roles of those individuals involved with a child, also give some time to think about the individuals who might be involved, but may not be obvious or may not be spoken about by the child because of fear such as bullies, individuals who might be exploiting them, criminally or sexually or individuals who they are in a relationship with.

Activity 5.9

Create a resource that will help you identify the people who may be involved in the lives of children. Include their role, whether they have any responsibilities and what their relationship with the child is. You might consider a number of questions you could ask. You might want to think about a table to complete, or a spider diagram, or a number of concentric circles. Be creative, think about how you would use your resource with different aged children, children with a disability, children from culturally diverse backgrounds, and those who identify as LGBT+.

This resource is something you could share with your Practice Educator during your placement. You could use this resource and reflect on your learning from its use.

Venue – including the setting, environment, location where the event, situation, circumstance occurred. This could include the home where the child is living, someone else's home such as a friend's or it might be a strangers, school and community. Venue might not be confined to the home, think about Bourdieu's (2003) (discussed in Chapter 3) 'field', the environment, the social and institutional places and spaces where children 'hang out'. When considering the field, also think about the hierarchical position of the child and that of others. The venue might also be virtual, online, for example social media or gaming.

Things to consider

The setting, environment, location where the event, situation, circumstance occurred is significant. Think about the relationship between the venue and the child. If it is the home environment, be specific noting the room; if outside of the home, identify where; if online, what social media platform. Additionally, you would need to record the time of day when the event occurred.

Case study

Eliana, aged 14, informs you that when she goes to a community activity, people are racist towards her. She is reluctant to tell you where this activity is, and who facilitates it, because she is frightened that you will go and talk to them, which will make things worse. It is important to Eliana that she keeps going because she enjoys the activity.

Activity 5.10

You need to find out where Eliana is going. Thinking about the language, characters and their roles, what questions do you ask Eliana?

The audience – this will include the individual or individuals that the child is talking to – their audience. The child's audience will include parents, carers, family, friends, teachers along with many other people. You will be a part of their audience. It's all about building the relationship with the child. There are times when they might tell you something to shock you, or something which might not be true, and they might be seeking attention, or telling you only part of what happened. You need to identify these different aspects, enable the child to feel comfortable in talking to you and believe them. You need to believe what they are telling you, until you have evidence, not hearsay, to the contrary. Once again, we observe the importance of communication skills. What the child is telling you, in their words, might be misunderstood, misinterpreted or they could be using a word in the wrong context. It is your responsibility to clarify your understanding, to explore what they mean and ensure you write down and record their words. They might be using words they have heard other people say or they might have been told what to say to you. Think about the language they are using, their under-standing of the language, explore their story, listen to what they are saying and what they are not saying.

Things to consider

How long have you known the child, is this your first meeting or have you started to build a relationship? If you have started to build a relationship, consider your previous discussions, has anything changed, for example a change of words, phrases, maybe the child is starting to feel they can talk to you and can share more. If it is the first meeting, you need to go back to the script and consider the purpose of your involvement, always listen, write down and record what they have said (Davies and Duckett, 2019). We also need to consider who they have previously spoken to and what they have told them. Here we are looking for consistency in the child's story.

The editing process – the child will edit, depending upon their cognitive ability, their communication, their language, their presentation of self, depending on the message they wish to convey. You need to listen to the child's story, their voice. You will need to explore what it is like for the child to live in that home, attend that school, live in that community. The child might only be telling you what they want you to hear or what they feel comfortable in sharing.

Things to consider

Whose story is the child sharing? Whose words? Whose influence? Who is editing what they say?

Reflecting on the seven scenarios above

You have explored the seven scenarios of the dramaturgical approach to reflection in respect to preparing to work with children. You have started to think about how you would engage children in discussions, the questions you might ask, your observations You have created a resource and an activity to support those discussions.

What if ...

Having reflected on the seven scenarios of the dramaturgical model and considered various elements of working with children, let's now consider a number of scenarios – these are 'what ifs'. The purpose of these 'what if' questions is to get you thinking, and reflecting on your approach, your discussion, and what you would do in this situation. Again, we are planning and preparing ourselves for professional practice. After each question write down your answer.

What if ...

1. A nine-year-old has asked you to keep a secret, what do you say?
2. A young person asks you for £10.00, what do you do?
3. You have arranged a home visit to talk to an 11-year-old. This is your third meeting with them. When you arrive, they are playing a game on the computer with three of their friends, what do you do?
4. A parent refuses to let you speak to their child alone.

Comment

Each scenario presents a different response. You might have considered more than one response for some of the questions and some of the questions might raise an ethical dilemma.

Question 1 – as a social worker, you should be building trusting relationships with children along with all other individuals you work with. Therefore, you should be open and honest. Imagine how a child would feel, they have asked you to keep a secret and you have agreed, you have promised, they then tell you something that requires you to share that information, take further action, or initiate court proceedings. How do you think the child would feel? Do you think they would trust you and tell you anything in the future? Be open and honest, say you cannot keep a secret because sometimes you have to tell other people and it is about keeping them safe.

Question 2 – this question presents an ethical dilemma; what do you do? Give the money or say no? Again, think about relationship building, trust and being open and honest. Here there might be more than one answer. Firstly, the answer is no, we should not be giving anybody money. Secondly, some social work teams do provide money for young people, for example for travel expenses. In these situations you would follow the policies and procedures. You need to be accountable and ensure you have made a record in the case notes. Thirdly, this might be an emergency situation, for example you are working with a young person who is moving towards independent living. It is late in the afternoon and you don't have time to return to the office. The young person wants some food. In this situation you could telephone your manager and request approval to give the young person the money or alternatively you could take the young person to the shop and buy some food for them. You keep the receipt and inform your manager as soon as possible. You record what you have done, and why, in the case notes. Remember: accountability – professionalism.

Question 3 – another ethical dilemma? Do you ask the young person to see them alone? Do you ask the friends to leave? Or do you rearrange the visit? In this situation you would most likely rearrange the visit. Consider for a moment that you ask them to leave their friends to join you – what do you think they would say? What do you think they would do? Do you think they would engage in a piece of work with you? Unless it is a safeguarding issue and they are at risk of significant harm, as discussed in the next chapter, you would rearrange.

Question 4 – the parent has parental responsibility and you need to talk to the child. You would need to discuss the purpose of your visit and the reason why you wish to talk to the child alone. Once again, we see the importance of the knowledge and understanding of the purpose of your involvement, the importance of communication and negotiation skills and a clear understanding of the legislative framework, policies and procedures.

Comment

Applying the dramaturgical model of reflection in this method facilitates reflection on how you might plan and prepare to work with children. Thinking about a variety of situations and circumstances, what to consider when working with children, and when planning such work why not create a number of 'what if' questions. This will help you have an understanding of the purpose of your involvement and think about some of the potential questions you might be asked or encounter. When on placement you could share these questions in supervision and explore them with your practice educator.

Chapter summary

In this chapter, we have explored some key aspects relating to childhood, children and young people. The focus has been on working with children in different situations and circumstances. We have identified the importance of open and honest communication and building trust. Recognising individuality and exploring all aspects of the child's life, the importance of capturing their voice, their experiences and their words. We have explored the importance of planning and preparing when working with children. The dramaturgical model of reflection has been used in relation to what we need to consider. The next chapter will begin to explore safeguarding including harm, risk and abuse.

Further reading

Parker, J and Ashencaen Crabtree, S (eds) (2020) *Human Growth and Development in Children and Young People.* Bristol: Policy Press.

Each chapter in this edited book provides a comprehensive exploration of human growth and development in children and young people. It analyses different theoretical and practice perspectives of human development. The book will benefit you not only as a student but also one that you will return to as a social worker.

Walker, J and Horner, H (2020) *Social Work and Human Development*, 6th edn. London: Sage/ Learning Matters.

This book focuses on human growth and development through the life course. The book covers children and young people which is invaluable but also adults. This will provide you with knowledge and understanding of adult perspectives of human development. This will be very useful when working with parents.

COVID-19 impact on children

Children in Lockdown: What Coronavirus Means for UK Children (2020) UNICEF-UK-Children. https://downloads.unicef.org.uk/wp-content/uploads/2020/04/Unicef-UK-Children-In-Lockdown-Coronavirus-Impacts-Snapshot.pdf

Holt, L and Murray, L (2021) Children and Covid 19 in the UK. *Children's Geographies*. https:// doi.org/10.1080/14733285.2021.1921699

Joseph Rowntree Foundation (2021) *UK Poverty 2020/21 The leading independent Report*. Available at: file:///C:/Users/rache/Downloads/uk_poverty_2020-21_0%20(2).pdf

National Learning and Work Institute (2021) *Facing the Future Employment Prospects for Young People After Coronavirus March 2021*. National Learning and Work Institute. Available at: file:///C:/Users/rache/Downloads/Updated%20Facing%20the%20future%20-%20 20employment%20prospects%20for%20young%20people%20after%20Coronavirus.pdf

NHS Digital and the Office for National Statistics (2020) *The Mental Health of Children and Young People in England 2020 Report*.

Parker, J and Veasy, K (2021) Universal credit, gender and structural abuse. *The Journal of Adult Protection*. https://doi.org/10.1108/JAP-05-2021-0018

The Princess Trust, Tesco and YouGov (2021) *The Prince's Trust Tesco Youth Index 2021*. The Princess Trust. Available at: file:///C:/Users/rache/Downloads/YOUTH_INDEX_2021%20Web %20Upload.pdf

Public Health England (2021) *Research and Analysis: Chapter 2 Employment and Income Spotlight*. Available at: https://www.gov.uk/government/publications/covid-19-mental-health-and-wellbeing-surveillance-spotlights/employment-and-income-spotlight

Public Health England (2021) *Research and Analysis: Chapter 4 of the Covid 19 Mental Health and Wellbeing Surveillance Report*. Available at: https://www.gov.uk/government/publications/covid-19-mental-health-and-wellbeing-surveillance-report/7-children-and-young-people

The Impact of Covid-19 on Children and Young People (2021) The Children's Society. Available at: https://www.childrenssociety.org.uk/sites/default/files/2021-01/the-impact-of-covid-19-on-children-and-young-people-briefing.pdf

Useful websites

NSPCC: https://www.nspcc.org.uk/keeping-children-safe/.

6

Safeguarding

It will also introduce you to the following standards as set out in the Social Work Subject Benchmark Statement (2019):

5.4 Service users and carers
5.10 Problem-solving skills
5.15 Communication skills
5.16 Skills in working with others

See Appendix 2 for a detailed description of these standards.

Introduction

Safeguarding is a significant aspect of social work and will be the focus of this chapter. Within this chapter you will see the importance of professionalism, values and ethics, integrating theory to practice and working with children and families. Here you will continue your journey, reflecting on what you have learnt so far and assimilating your knowledge and understanding of safeguarding. You will examine the meaning of safeguarding along with its many ambiguities and complexities. This will include exploring the terms harm, risk and abuse, making reference to the Children Act 1989. Drawing on the Working Together to Safeguard Children: A Guide to Inter-Agency Working to Safeguard and Promote the Welfare of Children (HM Government, 2020), the importance of an interprofessional and multi-agency approach to safeguarding children will be explained. We will examine the categories of abuse with an emphasis on neglect. A case study will be used to explore the question: is it a safeguarding issue? Scenarios of the dramaturgical approach to reflection, discussed in Chapter 1, will be used to reflect on safeguarding and social work practice.

What do we mean by safeguarding?

To gain an understanding of safeguarding, we first need to recognise what safeguarding is, and why safeguarding is so important in social work practice. Within children and families social work, this includes any form of abuse to children. The Working Together to Safeguard Children Guidance (HM Government, 2020), defines child abuse as:

A form of maltreatment of a child. Somebody may abuse or neglect a child by inflicting harm, or by failing to act to prevent harm. Children may be abused in a family or in an institutional or community setting by those known to them or, more rarely, by others. Abuse can take place wholly online, or technology may be used to facilitate offline abuse. Children may be abused by an adult or adults, or another child or children.

(HM Government, 2020, p. 106)

As we can see child abuse is a form of maltreatment, a significant role of the social worker is to protect children from harm. However, definitions of child abuse reflect the current values of society and may be different from those historically or in the future. Therefore, child abuse is constantly changing with societal values. Abuse can be on an individual, family or community level and a social worker needs a thorough understanding of safeguarding and associated factors. This is clearly articulated within all of the Professional Standards, the PCF and Knowledge and Skills Statement for Child and Family Practitioners. Safeguarding is associated with risk, harm and abuse in addition to many other things; see Figure 6.1.

Figure 6.1 Safeguarding factors

This is not an exhaustive list, but provides an overview of what you need to consider when thinking about safeguarding. You also need to think about the psychological impact on children's health and well-being. The impact of abuse can be so devastating that it affects their whole life. Safeguarding is also associated with prevention and protecting children; see Figure 6.2.

Figure 6.2 Safeguarding social work

We have already identified that social workers need to be aware of the factors associated with safeguarding in addition to familiarising themselves with the safeguarding legislation, policies and procedures. Such knowledge is essential in the understanding of the purpose of your involvement, accountability and in the assessment of risk. An essential component of safeguarding is working in partnership. Working in partnership with the child, the parents, the family along with colleagues and other professionals. It really is about working together. Here the importance of communication and interpersonal skills come to the fore.

Activity 6.1

Reflecting on the word 'safeguarding', write down your initial thoughts of what this word means to you.

Comments

What were your first thoughts? What words did you use? What influenced your thoughts? Did you consider any particular environment, situation or circumstance in relation to safeguarding?

Understanding safeguarding – the wider picture

We have already identified that safeguarding is multifaceted and requires an interdisciplinary approach. You will develop your knowledge and understanding of safeguarding policies and procedures along with becoming accustomed to the legislative framework. Your skills of professional curiosity, an investigative approach to questioning and exploring and analysing multi-perspectives from many different individuals will develop. This will include drawing pieces of information together and differentiating between facts, opinion and hearsay. As a social worker you must never become complacent and think that you know everything, but rather continue to develop your knowledge and skills in all areas of safeguarding. Here we recognise the importance of Bourdieu's (1977, 1984) cultural capital and social capital within social work practice, for instance continuing professional development and building social networks.

Safeguarding requires numerous skills including communication, observation, questioning, negotiation and navigating the many different relationships that children might have. The child's ecology of self, their PPCT (Bronfenbrenner, 1979/2005), as discussed in Chapter 3, is an array of interdependent relationships between the family including wider family members and friends and environments, fields (Bourdieu, 1984, 1991), such as the family home, school and community. Additionally, there are the relationships the child has online, for example social media or gaming. The child can influence, and be influenced by, these various relationships. Within these relationships and fields there are protective factors and risk factors. Protective factors might be the parents, extended family members, friends or school including a particular teacher, or club that the child attends. Risk factors could also be the same people and within the same fields. Within the family, home stress is a risk factor. Stress may be a result of a lack of communication, misunderstanding, misinterpretation, financial constraints such as unemployment or working poverty and the subsequent anxiety in relation to providing adequate provisions. There is also employment where there is a high level of stress associated with the role or the prospect of becoming unemployed. Housing is another potential risk factor. This could be linked to unemployment, welfare benefits and associated financial constraints/anxieties, working poverty or social housing provision or private landlord. Additionally, children are at significant risk where there is domestic abuse. The community might also be a source of stress for the parents, children or family. Children are at risk of abuse from outside of the family home, which will be discussed later in this chapter.

Living within a stressful environment could impact greatly on the child's development and place them at greater risk of abuse. Child development theories place the child within the context of the family and social functioning and here we can see how different fields (Bourdieu, 1991, 2003) can impact the development of their habitus and capitals (Bourdieu, 1977, 1984). It could be argued that a child's ecology of self can be severely affected by an abusive relationship in addition to the detrimental consequences in the development of their habitus and capitals (Bourdieu, 1977, 1984). Once again, we can recognise the importance of applying the theoretical constructs of Bronfenbrenner and Bourdieu to safeguarding practice. Through explorative questioning, the social worker can assess the engagement and interactivity of, and between, the relationships within the child's life and determine any potential risk. We will now examine these areas in greater detail.

Harm, risk and abuse

Safeguarding is about protecting children from harm, risk and abuse. We need to recognise and acknowledge that risks are present in everyday life, and they cannot be eliminated but diminished and, to some extent, managed. When we talk about harm, risk and abuse in a safeguarding context, we are referring to an absence of behaviour, which could be neglect, for example not providing adequate supervision of a child or alternatively an act of a behaviour such as physically hurting a child.

The Children Act 1989

When a Local Authority receives information that a child might be suffering, or is likely to suffer, significant harm, it is required by Section 47 of the Children Act 1989 to make enquiries. This is called a Section 47 investigation. This would follow a strategy meeting/discussion (Chisnell and Kelly, 2019; Davies and Duckett, 2019; Johns, 2020). The Section 47 investigation would be undertaken by a social worker who would complete an assessment. This assessment would be a multi-agency assessment, which will be discussed in the next chapter. The Children Act 1989 introduced the concept of significant harm as the threshold that justifies compulsory intervention in family life (Chisnell and

Kelly, 2019; Davies and Duckett, 2019; Johns, 2020). However, such intervention must be in the best interests of the child. The Children Act 1989 states that 'harm' means ill-treatment or the impairment of health or development including:

- 'development' means physical, intellectual, emotional, social or behavioural development,
- 'health' means physical or mental health,
- 'ill-treatment' includes sexual abuse and forms of ill-treatment which are not physical.

This definition was extended in the Adoption and Children Act 2002 to include: impairment suffered from seeing or hearing the ill-treatment of another. This has been included in the Domestic Abuse Act 2021.

Domestic abuse

Seeing and hearing the ill-treatment of others can have a devastating impact on children, placing them at risk of significant harm. For example, if a child attempts to intervene to protect the person from being hurt, or something is thrown and hits them. Alternatively, they may be deliberately harmed by the abuser. There is also the emotional impact on children and the potential of neglect. This impact can be with them throughout their lives. Social workers need to develop their knowledge and understanding of domestic abuse, including controlling and coercive behaviour, and the impact on children (HM Government, 2020). The Domestic Abuse Act 2021 includes a statutory definition of domestic abuse; as part of this Act, children will be regarded as victims of domestic violence if they see, hear or otherwise suffer the impact of abuse.

Working together to safeguard children

When there are concerns that a child has suffered significant harm, or is at risk of suffering significant harm, the social worker will undertake an assessment. The social worker, working in partnership with the family, will gather information from as many different sources as possible in order to protect the child, which will be explored in the next chapter. Safeguarding is multidimensional and the social worker does not work in isolation, but with the child, the parents, colleagues and other professionals. The Working Together to Safeguard Children: A Guide to Inter-Agency Working to Safeguard and Promote the Welfare of Children (HM Government, 2020) is a significant document that provides guidance in relation to working interprofessionally and applying a multi-agency approach, which will be referred to as 'the Guidance' for briefness. This is a key document within children and families social work and one that you will need to get familiar with. A suggestion would be that you read the Guidance, one chapter at a time, and at the end of each chapter reflect on what you have read and write a brief summary asking yourself:

- What is this chapter telling me?
- Why is this chapter important?
- What learning can I take from this chapter?
- How do I implement the Guidance in my practice?

This will help you gain a thorough knowledge and understanding of the Guidance and what safeguarding means. It is also worth noting that this Guidance is regularly updated so you need to be aware of the current version.

Activity 6.2

Read the Introduction (pp. 6–12) of the Working Together to Safeguard Children: A Guide to Inter-Agency Working to Safeguard and Promote the Welfare of Children (HM Government, 2020) guidance and write a brief reflection on why you think this is an important document.

Activity 6.3

Create a writing schedule, a table, of when you will read and reflect on the chapters of the Guidance. For example:

Chapter	Date
Chapter 1: Assessing need and providing help	

The chapters are long and therefore give yourself plenty of time to study them.

The Guidance places importance on partnership working. Safeguarding is not the sole responsibility of the social worker but is the responsibility of everyone that comes into contact with children. The Guidance states that 'safeguarding and promoting' the welfare of children is defined for the purposes of this guidance as:

- protecting children from maltreatment,
- preventing impairment of children's mental and physical health or development,
- ensuring that children grow up in circumstances consistent with the provision of safe and effective care,
- taking action to enable all children to have the best outcomes.

(HM Government, 2020, p. 6)

Information sharing

Information sharing includes the sharing of information where there are safeguarding and child protection concerns. It is important to note that 'The Data Protection Act 2018 and General Data Protection Regulations (GDPR) do not prevent the sharing of information for the purposes of keeping children safe. Fears about sharing information must not be allowed to stand in the way of the need to promote the welfare and protect the safety of children' (HM Government, 2020, p. 19) (there is also a 'myth-busting guide to information sharing', see HM Government, 2020, p. 21). As a social worker you will need to familiarise yourself with data protection legislation and the sharing of information. Placements are an excellent opportunity to seek out opportunities for training, identifying and reading policies relating to data protection, sharing information and confidentiality.

Scotland – National guidance for child protection

National guidance for child protection in Scotland (2014) sets out the essential principles that relate to child protection including Getting It Right for Every Child (GIRFEC) and the United Nations (UN) Convention on the Rights of the Child, the Children's Charter and the Framework for Standards. It describes what these principles and standards mean in practice. Paramount among these principles is that child protection must be seen within the wider context of supporting families and meeting children's needs. *GIRFEC* supports families by making sure children receive appropriate help and support, at the right time, from the right people.

The aim is to help children grow up feeling loved, safe and respected so that they can realise their full potential.

Wales – safeguarding children and young people

Social Services and Well-being Act (Wales) (2014) provides an overview of the safeguarding process, which includes the Working Together to Safeguard People, Vol. 5: Handling Individual Cases to Protect Children at Risk. Within these documents, reference is made to prevention and early help, identification of concerns and a duty to report these concerns to the Local Authority social services including the initiation of Section 47 enquiries under the Children Act 1989. There is an emphasis on immediate protection to keep children at risk of harm safe.

Northern Ireland – safeguarding children and young people

Co-operating to Safeguard Children and Young People in Northern Ireland (2017) provides the overarching policy for safeguarding children in the statutory, private, independent, community, voluntary and faith sectors. This policy outlines how communities, organisations and individuals must work both individually and in partnership to ensure children are safeguarded as effectively as possible. Within this policy the term 'safeguarding' is used in its widest sense and includes the promotion, prevention and protection for children's welfare and protection from harm.

Categories of abuse

Categories of significant harm include physical abuse, sexual abuse, neglect and emotional abuse. The follow definitions are taken from the Guidance (HM Government, 2020).

Physical abuse

A form of abuse which may involve hitting, shaking, throwing, poisoning, burning or scalding, drowning, suffocating or otherwise causing physical harm to a child. Physical harm may also be caused when a parent or carer fabricates the symptoms of, or deliberately induces, illness in a child.

(HM Government, 2020, p. 106)

Physical abuse is a deliberate act of abuse. This is usually referred to as a non-accidental injury inflicted by the caregiver. The social worker needs to determine whether any injury, to a child, is accidental or non-accidental. Accidental injuries might be looked at to determine whether neglect has occurred. In other words, whether the caregiver did not appropriately supervise the child.

Sexual abuse

Involves forcing or enticing a child or young person to take part in sexual activities, not necessarily involving a high level of violence, whether or not the child is aware of what is happening. The activities may involve physical contact, including assault by penetration (for example, rape or oral sex) or non-penetrative acts such as masturbation, kissing, rubbing and touching outside of clothing. They may also include non-contact activities, such as involving children in looking at, or in the production of, sexual images, watching sexual activities, encouraging children to behave in sexually inappropriate ways, or grooming a child in preparation for abuse. Sexual abuse can take place online, and technology can be used to facilitate offline abuse. Sexual abuse is not solely perpetrated by adult males. Women can also commit acts of sexual abuse, as can other children.

(HM Government, 2020, p. 107)

We need to consider where there have been incidents of individual's befriending children, online, in an attempt to get those children to remove their clothes and film or take images of themselves. These individuals are grooming children who are often threatened by them if they refuse. There have also been incidents where a young person has been in a relationship and their boyfriend or girlfriend has tried to force them to send images of themselves. This is referred to as 'sexting'. These are two examples of sexual abuse. It is against the law to take, send or redistribute images of anyone under the age of 18. The Child Exploitation and Online Protection Centre (CEOP) investigates cases of sexual abuse and grooming on the internet.

Neglect

The persistent failure to meet a child's basic physical and/or psychological needs, likely to result in the serious impairment of the child's health or development. Neglect may occur during pregnancy as a result of maternal substance abuse. Once a child is born, neglect may involve a parent or carer failing to: a. provide adequate food, clothing and shelter (including exclusion from home or abandonment) b. protect a child from physical and emotional harm or danger c. ensure adequate supervision (including the use of inadequate caregivers) d. ensure access to appropriate medical care or treatment It may also include neglect of, or unresponsiveness to, a child's basic emotional needs.

(HM Government, 2020, p. 108)

Evidence of neglect could be immediate, for example inadequate supervision by the caregiver resulting in a child being injured. This is an act of omission by the caregiver responsible for the child. The act of omission could be intentional or unintentional. This could occur inside or outside the family home, or leaving the child with someone else to look after them. There are many dangers within the home that could present a risk to a child. The question here is: is the child at risk of significant harm? The caregiver needs to ensure that any hazards, dangers or threats are minimised and the child is appropriately supervised. Neglect could also include the lack of basic care such as adequate nutrition and personal hygiene. The lack of care could have detrimental consequences on the child's health, well-being and development. There are also long-term consequences of neglect, which potentially impact the child throughout their life. The result of neglect could include cognitive, physical, emotional and/or social harm either immediately or in the future.

The National Society for the Prevention of Cruelty to Children (NSPCC) highlights four types of neglect. These are:

- **Physical neglect** – a child's basic needs, such as food, clothing or shelter, are not met or they aren't properly supervised or kept safe,
- **Educational neglect** – a parent doesn't ensure their child is given an education,
- **Emotional neglect** – a child doesn't get the nurture and stimulation they need. This could be through ignoring, humiliating, intimidating or isolating them,
- **Medical neglect** – a child isn't given proper health care. This includes dental care and refusing or ignoring medical recommendations.
  (https://www.nspcc.org.uk/what-is-child-abuse/types-of-abuse/neglect/)

Research by Friedman and Billick (2015) highlights the complexities of identifying neglect recognising that the reasons can be wide ranging and include parental stress resulting from poverty, parental alcohol and substance use, or parental illness. As highlighted above, neglect can be either intentional or unintentional and the social worker needs to be able to differentiate between the two and identify the risk and protective factors. The following three examples provide an illustration of the possibility of unintentional neglect. However, when we examine the definition of neglect above, we can see that the parents might not be providing adequate supervision. In the first two examples, support might be available to assist the parents, and in the third example the parent should be ensuring their children are appropriately supervised. Prioritising technology-related activities could place their children at risk. With regards to technology, for example, research by Gros et al. (2020) indicates that gaming addiction is increasing significantly. There are many associated factors with this addiction including distress if the individual is unable to play, depression if unable to play, in addition to:

fatalities have been associated with such extremely long periods of gaming; others may find themselves able to stop after a while, and indeed to punctuate their gaming with periods of work and/or academic activity, but nevertheless cannot get rid of their obsession with gaming and allow it to dominate their lives, possibly at the cost of previously treasured relationships, activities and ambitions.

(UK Rehab, https://www.uk-rehab.com/behavioural-addictions/gaming/)

Here we could say that technology runs along a continuum: at one end, technology-related activities could be interwoven within caring responsibilities with no detrimental effect and at the other end of the continuum, we have addiction such as gaming addiction that has the potential to leave children being unsupervised. There are also similar consequences associated with social media addiction and exercise addiction. An addiction is likely to place stress on the family relationships and potentially contribute towards financial hardship, ill health, and increases the risk of child abuse.

Three examples of potential unintentional neglect

Disability

Siblings of children with a disability may experience unintentional neglect. Many parents caring for a child with a disability report that caring requires much more time, parents are often more tired because of disrupted sleep, and a child with a disability may require increased levels of supervision. The intensity of caring often results in the siblings receiving inadequate supervision. This could lead to neglect, although this might be unintentional. Therefore, the social worker would need to differentiate between unintentional neglect and neglect. Here we see the importance of sensitive communication and assessment skills, whereby the social worker is not blaming or demeaning the parents, but ensuring that the children have not suffered or are at risk of suffering significant harm. Siblings of children with a disability may also provide care to their sibling. This also needs to be considered to ensure appropriate supervision.

Illness

Many children live with a parent with a life-limiting illness. Due to the illness the parent might not be able to provide adequate care thus resulting in unintentional neglect. The parent's illness may impact on them being able to provide basic care, adequate supervision or appropriate nutrition. The children might have poor school attendance or when in school be struggling to concentrate. The children might also be providing care for their parent in addition to looking after siblings. A social worker working with the family could refer the children to Young Carers for support. However, this referral needs to be made with sensitivity as they may not want to leave their parent or be seen as being different (Fearnley, 2012). A referral to Adults Services might provide additional support.

Technology

With increasing technological advances, people are working from home far more, which means that parents can be online working. There is also social media, gaming and physical exercise equipment all connected to the internet and available 7 days a week, 24 hours a day. When a parent is online, for whatever reason, there is significant potential for unintentional neglect. The questions to be asked are: are the children being adequately supervised, are they at risk of significant harm and are their basic needs being met?

Summary – three examples of unintentional neglect

The three examples provide circumstances where there might be unintentional neglect. The social worker in each of these situations would need to assess whether the child had suffered significant harm or was at risk of suffering significant harm (Children Act 1989). You would need to differentiate between unintentional neglect and neglect. Within the three examples, you could explore the parent's ecologies of self, discussed in Chapter 3. The importance here is communication and through explorative questioning identify what might be impacting on the parent's ability to parent. The definition of neglect states that it is the 'persistent failure to meet a child's basic physical and/or psychological needs, likely to result in the serious impairment of the child's health or development' (HM Government, 2020, p. 108). In the three examples above, we could ask ourselves what constitutes 'persistent failure'. Here again, reference can be made to Bronfenbrenner's (1979/2005) ecological framework, where we could explore the potential impact on the child's development – their PPCT. However, as we have already identified neglect could be as a result of inadequate supervision and thus placing the child at immediate risk of significant harm.

Emotional abuse

The persistent emotional maltreatment of a child such as to cause severe and persistent adverse effects on the child's emotional development. It may involve conveying to a child that they are worthless or unloved, inadequate, or valued only insofar as they meet the needs of another person. It may include not giving the child opportunities to express their views, deliberately silencing them or 'making fun' of what they say or how they communicate. It may feature age or developmentally inappropriate expectations being imposed on children. These may include interactions that are beyond a child's developmental capability, as well as overprotection and limitation of exploration and learning, or preventing the child participating in normal social interaction. It may involve seeing or hearing the ill-treatment of another. It may involve serious bullying (including cyber bullying), causing children frequently to feel frightened or in danger, or the exploitation or corruption of children. Some level of emotional abuse is involved in all types of maltreatment of a child, though it may occur alone.

(HM Government, 2020, p. 107)

Emotional abuse, alternatively referred to as psychological abuse, includes cognitive forms of abuse, as well as acts of omission, such as not providing emotional warmth to the child, and commission, for example doing something such as the parents ignoring the child. Emotional abuse may include:

- rejection,
- insulting, for example name calling,
- frightening,
- ignoring,
- humiliating,
- destroying or threatening to destroy personal belongings, for example removal of toys, games, clothes.

An important thing to consider when thinking about emotional abuse is whether it is persistent. Emotional abuse can have long-lasting consequences for the child and throughout adulthood. There is an interconnectedness between all forms of abuse. Additionally, there is an element of emotional abuse with all forms of abuse, but not necessarily the other way round. For example, physical abuse may include hitting; attached to this is the emotional aspect. The social worker's role is to ensure the safety and well-being of children.

Activity 6.4

Reflecting on the four categories of abuse, write down your answers to the following questions:

- What is meant by physical abuse?
- How could sexual abuse occur online?
- There are three children in the family and one child is frequently called names and excluded from family activities; is this emotional abuse? If so, why?
- A child, aged five, is frequently left at home unsupervised while their parents go to the shop; what category do you think this might be?
- You are concerned that the parents are neglecting their baby; who would you contact to gather further information?

For a thorough exploration of the categories of abuse see Davies and Duckett (2019) and for safeguarding Chisnell and Kelly (2019).

Working together guidance

The Guidance refers to a child-centred approach when safeguarding and promoting the welfare of the child. Such an approach means that the child's safety and well-being are the most important aspects when making decisions about their lives.

The principles of the Children Acts 1989 and 2004 state that the welfare of children is paramount and that they are best looked after within their families, with their parents playing a full part in their lives, unless compulsory intervention in family life is necessary (HM Government, 2020, p. 9). The Guidance provides a wealth of information and is a very useful resource, including (Table 6.1):

Table 6.1 The guidance – a resource

The Working Together to Safeguard Children: A Guide to Inter-Agency Working to Safeguard and Promote the Welfare of Children 2018 (HM Government, 2020)
• Information sharing – The Data Protection Act 2018 and General Data Protection Regulations (GDPR) and safeguarding (p. 18)
• Statutory requirements for children in need (p. 22)
• Homelessness Duty (p. 23)
• Appendix A: Glossary (p. 106)
• Domestic abuse definition (p. 110)
• Appendix B: Further sources of information (p. 112)
• Guidance issued by other government departments and agencies (p. 113)
• Guidance issued by external organisations (p. 114)

Assessment of risk outside the home

Assessment of risk outside the home was, in the 2018 Guidance, referred to as contextual safeguarding: 'contextual safeguarding is an approach to understanding and reacting to young people's experiences of exploitation and abuse situated within the wider community' (Frost, 2021, p. 133). Contextual safeguarding has subsequently changed to assessment of risk outside of the family home to encompass a broader definition including all forms of abuse, exploitation and teenage relationship abuse.

Activity 6.5

Thinking about children and young people when outside of the family home, how many areas of risk can you identify?

Comment

You might have thought of bullying, grooming or exploitation. Relationship abuse is another significant area irrespective of gender, ethnicity or sexual orientation. Within all of these situations, the young person might not wish to share their experiences with their parents or other adults; not sharing might present a risk in itself. Here we can see how the young person's ecologies of self, discussed in Chapter 3, along with their habitus and capitals, can be influenced or impacted upon by external forces. Such influences might result in changes in their relationships, for example with their parents, siblings, friends or teachers. Here we have an example of how the young person's microsystem is impacting upon the parent's ecosystem. This is an example of Bronfenbrenner's (1979/2005) exosystem, where the parent does not have direct contact with the external source but there is a direct impact on their microsystem. As the social worker working with the young person, you could explore any changes in behaviour, mood or demeanour. Working with the parents, you could explore their observations of any changes. In Chapter 3, we discussed the chronosystem which relates to time; within your discussion you could use a timeline (Parker, 2021) to explore any changes that have occurred and over what period.

Criminal exploitation

Criminal exploitation is when a child or young person is groomed, abused or manipulated to do something on behalf of another individual or individuals. The child or young person is usually provided with gifts, alcohol or drugs followed with an expectation to do something, for the other person, that is illegal. Fear of reprisal and repercussion is part of the exploitation, for example if they tell anyone what they are doing:

> *Child criminal exploitation is common in county lines and occurs where an individual or group takes advantage of an imbalance of power to coerce, control, manipulate or deceive a child or young person under the age of 18. The victim may have been criminally exploited even if the activity appears consensual. Child criminal exploitation does not always involve physical contact; it can also occur through the use of technology.*

(Home Office, 2020)

Sexual exploitation

Sexual exploitation is similar to criminal exploitation in that children and young people are groomed, abused or manipulated to do something on behalf of another individual or individuals; however, this includes some form of sexual activity. All children and young people are at risk of being groomed and child sexual exploitation irrespective of their gender, ethnicity or sexuality or whether they are living with their parents or are children in care. Research identified that many young people are frightened to tell anyone, for fear of repercussions from the abusers, and if they do, they will not be believed. An investigation into child sexual abuse identified that:

> *In just over a third of cases, children affected by sexual exploitation were previously known to services because of child protection and child neglect. There was a history of domestic*

violence in 46% of cases. Truancy and school refusal were recorded in 63% of cases and 63% of children had been reported missing more than once.

(Jay, 2014, p. 32)

The following research summary provides an example of how abuse outside the family might occur.

Research summary

Research undertaken by Melrose (2013) identified that many young women are placed under pressure to engage in sexual activity as a result of being 'duped or manipulated by older males' (p. 161). Melrose (2013) observed that young women were invited to parties with the expectation that they would engage in sexual activity with many different men. It is the 'emotional vulnerability' of these young women that drives their 'willing acceptance' to attend parties to 'achieve popularity' (Melrose, 2013, p. 163). The vulnerability of these young women, many living within a hostel environment, often isolated, disowned or rejected by their parents, makes them susceptible to engaging in such activities. The persistent neglect by parents is likely to have long-term consequences including feelings of worthlessness, being powerless and undeserving of anything better and thus an acceptance of how they are treated.

Comment

The commonalities of criminal and sexual exploitation are that all children and young people are at risk of grooming, abuse and manipulation outside the home. Within the research summary, grooming starts with the invitation to the party; abuse is the expectation of engagement in sexual activity; and manipulation could be playing on the young women's vulnerability, desire to be popular and resulting in psychological abuse. Young people are unlikely to share their experiences, which places them at greater risk. Research into sexual exploitation (Jay, 2014) indicates that many young people felt that they were not believed when they spoke to professionals. As social workers we need to ensure that we are listening to young people, are enabling them to have a voice and we make sure that they are listened to. This includes the words they use, language and non-verbal communication including body language.

Activity 6.6

You are meeting a young person for the first time, their parent informs you that they are regularly absent from school and staying out late at night, you think they are being exploited. How might you approach your discussion with the young person?

Comment

Think about the dramaturgical approach to reflection, that we explored in Chapter 1. Reflect on how you would prepare for this discussion. The script is that the young person might be being exploited; consider the language you will use, the words. Who the characters/actors are in this scenario – what questions will you use to explore these characters and what their roles are? Consider the venue where you will talk to this young person – think about the venue where they feel safe and comfortable. Also consider confidentiality ensuring that no one else can hear the discussion. Think about who you will share the information with and how will you edit that information.

Is it a safeguarding issue?

As we have identified, safeguarding is multidimensional: it is about exploring the actions and interactions of, and between, various relationships and the impact of such on the child. Safeguarding children is about working collaboratively to protect them from harm and promote their health, well-being and development (Frost, 2021; Keeling and Goosey, 2020). Exploring relationships and working collaboratively includes the children, parents and wider family members in addition to other professionals. As an example, let's revisit the family in Case Study 1 in Chapter 2.

Case study

You arrive at the family home to undertake an assessment, you observe three puppies, the floor is wet and you observe a baby and a three-year-old playing on the living room floor. Previously we discussed this in relation to assumptions and how such assumptions might influence our decision-making.

Here the question is: 'Is this a safeguarding issue?'

The answer is possibly. Let's say that the initial referral was from the health visitor who had concerns about the children and the puppies. Exploring these concerns with the health visitor would provide further information. Here is where communication and questioning are so important along with having a thorough understanding of the purpose of the assessment. The initial referral and concerns would determine the assessment and any subsequent intervention. If the wet floor was caused by animal urine or there were dog faeces on the floor, then this, potentially, would be a safeguarding issue. We would also want to see if there were any connections between our observations of a wet floor and those of the health visitor. We need to consider the health and well-being of the baby and the three-year-old playing on the floor. Revisiting the Children Act 1989, and in particular reference to significant harm and the impairment of health or development (Children Act 1989), we can see that a wet floor caused by animal urine could place the children at risk and likely to suffer significant harm. A contributory factor would be whether the children were exposed to it.

Activity 6.7

If this was a safeguarding issue, what category of abuse would you be considering? And why?

Comment

What we can see here are the complexities of safeguarding. The question of whether this constitutes a safeguarding issue is determined by a number of factors. We could say yes, because research (Penakalapati et al., 2017) clearly indicates that animal urine and faeces can cause significant health problems in humans. On the other hand, we could say no because the parents might be aware of such health implications and therefore, maintain a level of hygiene to ensure the children are not at risk. However, the health visitor reported their concerns and you have both observed a wet floor. When we look at the four categories of abuse we can see, and taking into consideration this is your first visit, there is no evidence of physical or sexual abuse. This leaves the two remaining categories: neglect and emotional abuse. Emotional abuse is a category of abuse that can be in its own right. It is also the only category of abuse that is associated with other forms of abuse. Therefore, we would first look at neglect. The definition of neglect, discussed previously in this chapter, identifies the key elements for this situation are firstly, the possible act of omission in relation to adequate and appropriate care of the children, secondly, we need to ask ourselves is there 'persistent failure'. However, this failure needs to result in the serious impairment of the children's health or development, which raises the question of: do two observations equate to 'persistent failure'? It is unlikely you will have the evidence to demonstrate a safeguarding issue during the first visit. However, while in the family home, you need to apply your skills of observation and communication. What do you see, a baby and three-year-old child playing on the floor? Let's consider the baby: firstly you need to consider the age of the baby, is it mobile, crawling, able to stand or walk. When you see the baby, is there 'free movement', or restrictions or signs of pain in the facial expressions? How much of the baby can you see, how much is covered by clothing? Again, with the three-year-old, what do you see? Are they moving or mobile, how much of the child is visible, are they communicative? The question that needs to be answered is, are you seeing the children and the answer is simply 'yes', you are seeing them. However:

What is not visible? What aspect of the body would be important to see? Is there enough (bodily) information to make a defensible decision? Our understanding of the body is not only socially constructed and situated within cultural norms, but is also compressed by the kind of visual practices available to us. In other words, we cannot always see what we need to know – it is not always literally in front of us.

(Philips, 2014, p. 2266)

You need to be aware of your own biases and not make assumptions, or look for something that might simply be an accident by the puppies, but at the same time, we need to ensure that the children are safe and well. Any decision you make needs to be defendable; a defensible decision is one which is supported with evidence (Killick and Taylor, 2020). In Chapter 1, we said that observations were tacit knowledge and therefore would not provide factual evidence; however, in Case Study 1, you have observed that the floor is wet and thus you are able to state, 'during my visit to (name of family, date, time) I observed that the floor was wet', in your assessment. The question to be asked here is: Do you have any evidence of what was on the floor to be making it wet? You are now beginning to understand the complexities of safeguarding.

Dramaturgical approach to reflection

The dramaturgical approach to reflection, discussed in Chapter 1, will be used to reflect on how we might work with the parents in this situation. Here we will explore two scenarios of this model: language and audience.

Language – in preparation for the initial visit, and considering what information you have, you need to consider the language you might use. You do not know this family; there has been no prior involvement with Children's Services. What information do you need to know? The language used to engage the parents in discussion needs to reflect the potential seriousness of the situation, but as discussed in Chapter 2, you should not make assumptions. Also think about the sensitivity of this matter; it might be embarrassing for the parents.

Activity 6.8

What further information would you like to know about the situation? Thinking about language, what questions would you ask to gather the information? Would you like to know anything else about the children? Why? And why do you need to know? What questions would you ask?

Audience – the audience is the individuals you are working with; in Case Study 1, these would be parents, the health visitor and your team manager. Think about who else might be involved in the family and who could provide further information.

Activity 6.9

Would you discuss this situation with the parents individually or together? Why?

Activity 6.10

A parent does not take their eight-year-old to the dentist for a routine dental appointment; is this a safeguarding issue?

Comment

You might say no, there are many reasons why a parent misses a child's dental appointment. This is not necessarily a safeguarding issue; however, we need to explore the wider perspective. Further, if the dentist has informed Children's Services that the child has missed an appointment, we would need to discuss their concerns. With reference to the Children Act 1989, we need to consider whether the child has suffered significant harm or if the child is at risk of suffering significant harm. During the discussions with the parent, in addition to the dentist, we would gather information about the child's general health and well-being, frequency of previous visits along with exploring whether other health appointments had been missed. Missed appointments could be a sign of neglect. The key word here is 'persistent'. This was highlighted previously in this chapter as medical neglect (NSPCC).

At first glance a missed dental appointment does not warrant a referral to Children's Services; however, when we explore the wider perspective, we can see that there is much more we need to know before we can dismiss it entirely. We would need to know the dentist's concerns and the frequency of missed appointments:

All healthcare organisations and healthcare providers have a duty outlined in legislation, regardless of who the commissioner is, to make arrangements to safeguard and promote the welfare of children and young people, and to co-operate with other agencies to protect individual children and young people from harm.

(Anon, 2019, p. 12)

Dentists have an opportunity, like other professionals, to talk to children along with observing their health and well-being. They also have the opportunity to talk to parents and observe the interactions between children and their parents. The dentist along with other members of their team 'are in a position where they may observe the signs of child abuse and neglect, or hear something that causes them concern about a child' (Harris et al., 2009, p. 11). They have a responsibility to safeguard children if they have concerns:

Dental neglect and missed appointments are the most common reasons for dentists to make child protection referrals. They cause concern because they:

- *may be an alerting feature that a child or young person is being neglected,*
- *are often found when a child has died or been seriously harmed by maltreatment, when a 'serious case review' is conducted.*

(Harris and Kirby, 2019, p. 3)

Harris and Kirby (2019) encourage us to use 'was not brought' rather than 'did not attend' (p. 3). They want professionals to consider the situation from the child's perspective and identify the impact on the child's well-being. Considering this perspective, and acknowledging parental responsibility, we can see that it is the parent's responsibility to look after their children including their health and well-being. Therefore, we can see it is not the child who did not attend, but rather the parent who did not take the child to their appointment thus 'was not brought'. However, does the situation change if we have a young person? Parents are responsible for children up to their 18th birthday (Children Act 1989). Consider a young person aged 16 or 17; how would they feel being taken to the dentist by their parent? This would depend on the individual, situation and circumstances. Some young people would be happy, some not and would prefer to go alone. We also need to consider Fraser Competence (following the Gillick case – see Johns, 2020), where the competence of the young person to make informed decisions should be taken into consideration. We also need to consider the Children Act 1989 where the wishes and feelings of the child need to be taken into consideration.

Dramaturgical model of reflection

The dramaturgical model of reflection, discussed in Chapter 1, will be used to reflect on how we might work with the parents in this situation. Here we will explore two scenarios of this model of reflection: the script and the venue.

The script – the script places the event, situation, circumstance into context. Here we have a child who has missed a dental appointment, why is this significant? Only the dentist can provide such information. However, we also need to consider the parent's perspective. Once again, we see the importance of communication skills, applying an investigatory approach of questioning to ascertain the significance while remaining professional and working collaboratively with the dentist. You would consider the child's health and well-being, their development and their social presentation. Thought needs to be given to whether the parents are meeting the child's basic care.

Activity 6.11

What questions would you ask the dentist? The parent? The child?

Venue – the referral has come from the dentist and therefore the dental surgery is the initial venue. There is also the family home. When undertaking the assessment, you might also consider contacting the school. School is important and could provide information in relation to the child's attendance, presentation and general well-being. Thus, various venues might be incorporated within an assessment to provide a wider perspective about the child's life.

Comment

What you will be assessing is whether the child has suffered, or is at risk of suffering significant harm. Gathering further information, including from the parents, will provide valuable information in relation to the 'persistence' of the care provided to the child. The gathering of further information is important as it enables you to make an informed decision.

Chapter summary

This chapter provides an overview of safeguarding. As we can see, social workers need to have a thorough understanding of what safeguarding means, the legislative framework and the importance of applying an interprofessional and multi-agency approach. The social worker's role is to initially establish whether the child has suffered or is likely to suffer significant harm or is at risk of significant harm and whether abuse has taken place. They are responsible for preventing, protecting and intervening when it is necessary to safeguard a child. As identified, safeguarding is complex, multifaceted and at times, what might appear to be a simple case might be more serious. This may feel very daunting as you begin your journey through the social work course. However, as you begin to develop your knowledge and understanding through experience, it will become less daunting. In the next chapter, we will begin to explore the assessment process.

Further reading

Frost, N (2021) *Safeguarding Children and Young People: A Guide for Professionals Working Together.* London: Sage.

This book provides a history of child protection and understanding child abuse and child protection. The book is a comprehensive account of safeguarding, the demands, issues and complexities. It explores the wider social, political and policy context of safeguarding along with developing knowledge, skills and understanding of safeguarding within a wider context such as contextual safeguarding.

Johns, R (2020) *Using the Law in Social Work*, 8th edn. London: Sage/Learning Matters.

This comprehensive introductory book provides an overview of using the law in social work. This will be a good reference throughout your studies and when qualified.

Keeling, J and Goosey, D (2020) *Safeguarding Across the Life Span*. London: Sage.

This book focuses on safeguarding across the lifespan. The book explores the overlapping safeguarding concerns throughout the age continuum. It examines theories for safeguarding practice and the principles of safeguarding. The legislative framework is covered including safeguarding children and young people from online danger.

Useful websites

Gov.UK: https://www.gov.uk/government/publications/working-together-to-safeguard-children–2

7

Assessments

See Appendix 1 for the Professional Capabilities Framework Fan and a description of the nine domains.

It will also introduce you to the following standards as set out in the Social Work Subject Benchmark Statement (2019):

5.4 Service users and carers
5.10 Problem-solving skills
5.15 Communication skills
5.16 Skills in working with others
5.17 Skills in personal and professional development

See Appendix 2 for a detailed description of these standards.

Introduction

Undertaking assessments is multidimensional and incorporated within everything a social worker does. In this chapter, you will explore the assessment as a process rather than a single event. The fundamental components of the assessment process will be examined. Through this examination, you will specifically develop your knowledge and understanding of the importance of observations. The Assessment Framework (HM Government, 2020) will be introduced and explored through the theoretical constructs of Bronfenbrenner and Bourdieu. You will consider how these two theories contribute towards the undertaking of assessments, relationship building and provide a wider perspective of the situation and circumstances of an individual's life. You will be introduced to some assessment tools that facilitate social workers in identifying, supporting and working with children and parents.

Assessment as a process

Assessments are multidimensional and comprise of the application of different knowledge, skills and approaches of working. These will be explored as we work our way through this chapter. Assessments should be thought of in the context of the family, their past and present, their journey to where they are today and include their situation and circumstances individually and collectively. Assessments should be strengths based and culturally representative. When we think about assessments, we need to consider the undertaking of the assessment as a process rather than a single event: 'assessment is a purposeful, systematic, collaborative process of information gathering which supports analysis, recommendations and shared decision making' (Killick and Taylor, 2020, p. 5). Many assessments are completed in a single home visit; nevertheless, as we progress through the chapter, we will see that the single visit is only part of the process.

Purpose of the assessment

The Working Together to Safeguard Children Guidance (HM Government, 2020), discussed in Chapter 6, clearly states that:

Whatever the legislation the child is assessed under, the purpose of the assessment is always:

- *to gather important information about a child and family,*
- *to analyse their needs and/or the nature and level of any risk and harm being suffered by the child,*
- *to decide whether the child is a child in need (section 17) or is suffering or likely to suffer significant harm (section 47),*
- *to provide support to address those needs to improve the child's outcomes and welfare and where necessary to make them safe.*

(HM Government, 2020, p. 26)

When we consider the PCF Super Domains Purpose, Practice, Impact, we can see how these provide a structure to guide our practice.

Purpose

As a social worker you should have a thorough understanding of the purpose of the assessment you are about to undertake (Parker, 2020). This is noted in all four nations of the UK's Professional Standards and the KSS. Prior to undertaking an assessment, you should ask yourself 'what is the purpose of this assessment' and question 'why am I doing this assessment'. Such self-questioning will enable you to understand the reason for your involvement and what information you need and why. Getting into the habit of questioning yourself, with every assessment, is part of the planning and preparation work required not only for good professional practice, but also ethical practice. In Chapter 1, we identified the foundations of professional social work practice – see Figure 1.5 along with Figure 2.2 from Chapter 2. Such habits will also be very helpful when you don't have that preparation time and you need to complete an urgent assessment. The questions will be at the forefront of your mind, and you will be asking yourself those questions and considering the answers during the journey to undertake the assessment. Additionally, all assessments should include an assessment of risk (Calder and Archer, 2015; Killick and Taylor, 2020).

Practice

Practice relates to how you work with individuals, adults, children, colleagues and other professionals. When you work with individuals, your practice should always be underpinned by social work values and ethics, discussed in Chapter 2, in addition to applying an ethical approach in your judgements and decision-making (Dykes, 2019; Killick and Taylor, 2020). Assessments should be based on factual evidence and not hearsay along with partnership working and interventions that encourage active participation (Diaz, 2020). The majority of assessments undertaken, but not all, are to determine whether the child has suffered or is likely to suffer significant harm along with identifying whether they are at risk. Some assessments are to establish whether the child meets the eligibility criteria for support such as respite. All assessments should include the assessment of risk including:

- assessing actual or potential risk: in addition to immediate risk, there is long-term risk, for example the persistent failure to meet a child's basic needs such as neglect or emotional abuse. Assessment and intervention should therefore be focused on the family as key to understanding the dimensions of child abuse,
- risk analysis: an ongoing process during the assessment that informs the decision-making and intervention,
- management of risk: including planning, short- and long-term protection, and ensuring the child's health, well-being and development.

It is essential that the child's voice is listened to, their story is heard and is articulated throughout the assessment. When writing the assessment, think about, what is it like for the child to live in their home environment, in that situation and in those circumstances. You should be enabling them to share their journey and their story and include their words in your assessment.

Impact

Impact relates to the difference your practice makes. What difference did you make for the child? You need to be reviewing your practice regularly with the child, parents and during supervision with our manager/supervisor to ensure that you are acting in the best interest of the child. You should be asking yourself: what difference is my involvement making to protect and support the child? You should be working in partnership with the parents and other professionals, such as midwives, health visitors, teachers and the police along with making referrals to other agencies to provide additional support. Here you should be asking yourself: is the intervention working? And how do I know I am making a difference? You should be evaluating your work, working with parents and reviewing your work to ensure the right intervention is being applied. It is very important that if the intervention is not working, you need to change it and apply a different approach while continuing to working in partnership with the parents. Additionally, you need to reflect on your practice, learn from your experiences and apply the new learning into practice. You also need to be reflexive and consider the impact of your presence, be aware of your biases and not make assumptions. The question is: Does social work work? And that is the importance of reviewing your work, seeking feedback and evaluating any support or interventions.

Assessment and the professional standards

There are links between undertaking assessments and the Professional Standards (SWE); Practice Guidance (Wales); Codes of Practice for Social Service Workers and Employers

(Scottish Social Service Council); and the Standards of Conduct and Practice for Social Workers (Northern Ireland), as outlined in Chapter 1, and in Table 1.1 and the PCF and KSS. The commonalities include the importance of communication, values and ethics, building, developing, maintaining and ending relationships, working in partnership with families, parents, children and young people including promoting the rights and interests of individuals. Additionally, the assessment process necessitates an interprofessional and multi-agency approach.

The components of the assessment

Following the initial considerations of undertaking assessments, you will now look at what the assessment process comprises. These are: the initial referral, gathering of information, analysing information and decision-making, feedback loops – A and B, and C – short-term decision-making and protection. Although there are many different types of assessment, fundamentally the components remain the same. The purpose of the assessment might be different, but it should be viewed as a process. Let's explore the components of the assessment; see Figure 7.1.

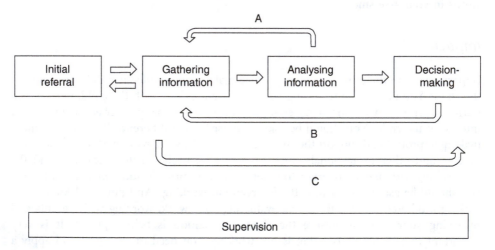

Figure 7.1 The assessment process

Within Figure 7.1, you can see the four main components along with elements A, B and C. 'A' illustrates a reflective feedback loop. You have gathered and coherently organised the information and during the analysis you identify unanswered questions, further information is required and maybe some clarity to ensure the assessment is factual. This takes us back to the gathering of information. Likewise, 'B' illustrates a reflective feedback loop during decision-making, which again, takes us to the gathering of information, followed by analysing information and returning to decision-making. Such reflection in 'A' and 'B' should enable an ethical assessment, subsequent professional judgement and decision-making. C shows how sometimes a short-term decision is required to protect the child(ren), or alternatively a referral to a parenting programme, although the assessment is ongoing. Figure 7.1 illustrates how the undertaking of an assessment is a process and not a single event. Even when undertaking an assessment during a single home visit, you should still be gathering information, organising, analysing and making a decision. Supervision spans all elements to support the social worker, ensure accountability, facilitate critical analysis and reflection. In Chapters 1 and 2, we identified the foundations of professional social work practice – see Figures 1.5 and 2.2, within the assessment process we are applying these foundations in practice.

Initial referral

The initial referral initiates the assessment process. The referral could be a self-referral, meaning that an individual, for example an adult, parent, carer, child or young person has referred themselves. They have brought themselves, for whatever reason, to the attention of Children's Services. Examples of self-referral include the need for support, to express concerns, or parental/young person relationship breakdown. Young people frequently refer themselves as homeless; they have been 'kicked out' by their parents. Initial referrals also come from professionals, for example from within health and education.

Activity 7.1

How many professionals can you think of that might make a referral?

Comment

Initial referrals can be made by anyone who is concerned about the safety, health and well-being of a child. You may have included midwives, health visitors and general practitioners (GPs), dentists, head teachers and the designated child protection leads within schools. The initial referral might contain detailed information; on the other hand, the information may be sparse and require further clarification.

Gathering information

Following the allocation of the referral to the social worker, the social worker will begin gathering and organising the information. The referral will have been made to the Multi-Agency Safeguarding Hub (MASH) Team (Home Office, 2014). The MASH Team triages referrals, makes initial enquiries, gathers further information, makes decisions in relation to risk and forwards the referral to the appropriate service provision. If a child is at risk, or has suffered significant harm (Children Act 1989), a Section 47 enquiry (Children Act 1989) will be undertaken. A referral requesting support is likely to be directed to the

Early Intervention Team. Some referrals to the early intervention team might require a Section 47 enquiry and thus a subsequent referral will be made. For some referrals, there will be no further action. Depending on the risk or likelihood of risk, the social worker will need to decide the urgency of arranging an initial visit to the family home. The Children Act 1989 and Working Together Guidelines (HM Government, 2020) clearly state the importance of working in partnership with parents. Parents must be informed of all stages of the assessment. Information for the assessment will be gathered from as many different sources as possible. The Working Together Guidelines (HM Government, 2020), explored in Chapter 6, provides guidance on inter-agency working, including sharing of information and the Data Protection Act 2018.

During the assessment process, there might be several discussions with the referrer; hence, in Figure 7.1, there are two arrows, between the initial referral and gathering information, highlighting that two-way dialogue is required. When you gather any information from another professional, you need to clarify that you have understood what has been said and any action that has been agreed. Additionally, and very importantly, you need to ask the professional to provide either a written statement or report with the information they have shared. You need this as a record of your discussion. This evidence may be required in the event of going to court. The gathering of information is ongoing throughout the assessment process and therefore needs to be organised coherently. The social worker needs to ensure that all information is current, relevant and accurate.

Skills for gathering information

Gathering information is a skill that will develop with practice and experience. When gathering information, you need to build and develop your communication skills. This includes developing your listening skills, for example, listening to what has been said and also being aware of what has not been said and by whom. Listening is very important in a different sense too, for example when you are on the telephone, what can you hear in the background? When in the family home, what can you hear? What can you not hear? What noises are present? When thinking about communication skills, you also need to think about how you will engage individuals in conversations and how you will use questions to explore, and clarify your understanding of what has been said. This builds on the importance of communication which we explored in Chapter 1.

Activity 7.2

As you are reading this, what can you hear? What noises can you hear? How do these impact on what you are doing?
Now think about how you would listen when undertaking an assessment, what would you hear that might offer insight into the situation and circumstances, are there noises that may distract your attention, are there things that you don't want to hear?

The importance of observations

Observation skills are essential in social work practice.

Activity 7.3

Stop what you are doing and take a few moments to look around you; what can you see? What can you hear?
Now look again; what can you see? What can you hear? Can you see, or hear, anything that you did not see, or hear, the first time?

Within your assessment, you need to observe the parent–child interactions. Is the parent interacting with their child and how? Is the child interacting with their parents and how? Remember that interactive communication could be verbal or non-verbal; what interactions are you observing? Are there toys available and accessible for the child, and if so, are they playing with them? How are they playing with them? Do they look comfortable playing with the toys? This might sound strange, but sometimes toys may have been placed to give the impression that the parent is providing age-appropriate activities and stimulation for their child. Such placing is referred to as disguised compliance. Disguised compliance is where the parent gives the impression, whether within the family home or through discussion, that they are providing for their children or doing what the social worker has asked, or what they want the social worker to see. Thinking about the Case Study in Chapter 6, we need to consider what is visible and what is not visible, what the child is doing and what the child is not doing and what they are saying and what they are not saying. Referring to Goffman, Chapter 1, what performance is the parents giving, how have they set the scene, and what don't they want us to see? Philips (2014) explores dance choreography in relation to seeing children and their bodily movement and how this might help to 'see' the child (see Table 7.1).

In Table 7.1, we can see how the social worker's observations, and their understanding of child development can support their assessment. The questions, proposed by Philips (2014) are for the social worker to consider. They are questions that the social worker should be asking themselves, both prior to and during their work with the family. Using these questions as prompts, they can explore the situation and circumstances through observation. These questions and observations are important in the assessment process as they enable the social worker to complete the process with much more rigour. Therefore, this self-questioning will support the completion of a thorough assessment.

Questions suggested by Philips (2014) are: What do I need to look for? How will I do so? These questions could form part of the planning of the assessment and therefore become integral to the social worker's thinking about 'what is the purpose of the assessment'. The 'what do I notice', is fundamental to the assessment and here you should be using all our senses. It is not just about what you see, but also what you hear and smell. You need to be asking yourself who initiates, shapes and invites me to what I see what is not available to me. Here you can see the importance of critical thinking through questioning your observations. Additionally, this includes the child's and parent's voice, their verbal and non-verbal communication including body language. You need to be consistently evaluating the situation, thinking about, for example who placed the toys next to the child. Has the parent placed them there and therefore invited me, as the social worker, to see a range of toys for the child to play with? They might have positioned themselves next to the child to suggest the provision of emotional warmth or making sure that the toys are safe and age appropriate. This relates to the question 'what is not available to me?'. Another question to ask ourselves is 'what am I afraid to see?' Here you could refer to Goffman (1959/1990), discussed in Chapter 1, and ask yourself: what performance are the parents giving, how have they set the scene, and what don't they want me to see? Additionally, what performance are the children giving?

Table 7.1 Questions offered by dance choreography

Epistemological encounters	Practice encounters
What are my seeing practices?	What do I need to look for? How will I do so?
	What do I notice?
	How do I want to be seen?
	Who initiates and shapes my seeing – both what I see and how I see?
	Who invites that seeing? What am I shown? What is not available to me?
How do I understand the body?	Can I see the child's everyday life?
How bodies communicate?	Can I see bodily effort? Pedestrian movement?
	What am I afraid to see?

Philips, R. C. (2014) 'Seeing the Child' beyond the Literal: Considering Dance Choreography and the Body in Child Welfare and Protection, *British Journal of Social Work*, 44: 2254–2271 by permission of Oxford University Press.

Figure 7.2 provides a visual representation of how we could consider these questions. The line indicates what we are being told, what we can see and observe and what we are being directed to see and hear. Below the line indicates what we can't see, what we are not being told, not shown, which raises the question, what do we need to know. Referring to Goffman, Chapter 1, we could say that above the line is the front stage and below the line is the back stage. The social worker represents the audience and only sees the performance – the front stage. However, what is happening back stage – are the children at risk?

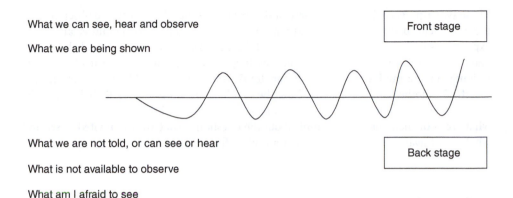

What we can see, hear and observe

What we are being shown

What we are not told, or can see or hear

What is not available to observe

What am I afraid to see

Front stage

Back stage

Figure 7.2 A visual representation of how we could consider the questions in Table 7.1

Revisiting Case study 1, Chapter 2 and Chapter 6

Activity 7.4

Revisit Case Study 1, Chapter 2 and Chapter 6, and refamiliarise yourself with the case study.

Case study

You arrive at the family home to undertake the assessment. This is your first visit. You observe three puppies, the floor is wet and you observe a baby and a three-year-old playing on the living room floor. The health visitor had informed you that when they had visited, the floor was wet. Let's reconsider this case study by exploring what is, and what might be, observed and the questions posed in Table 7.1.

You arrive at the family home where the parents greet you with a warm welcome. You are invited to sit down. You have observed the floor is wet and that the children are playing on the living room floor. The floor is wood and the children are on a rug.

You can see that these initial observations provide a lot of information. This information needs to be recorded within your case notes. Consider the questions in Table 7.1, who has initiated and shaped what you are observing? The parents? Who has invited what you are seeing? The parents? What is not available to you? What would you like to see? Thinking about the children, can you see their everyday life? This is a difficult question, however, what do you see, a baby and a three-year-old. Reflecting on your previous experience, and your knowledge and understanding of child development, what would you expect these children to be doing? Can you see bodily effort? Pedestrian movement?

These two aspects could have a variety of different meanings. What you are observing are the arms, legs, bodily movement and with ease, without stiffness or jerkiness, and facial expressions such as smiling and laughing (Philips, 2014). Ask yourself: if the baby was in pain, would they be gurgling or smiling as they moved? Is the three-year-old playing, walking, talking and engaging with the toys? Are the two children communicating together? Another consideration is how the children are dressed. Are their bodies fully clothed or dressed appropriately? For example, if it is cold and they are not fully clothed, what are your thoughts? Again, think about the questions, what are you invited to see and what is not available. And finally, what are you afraid to see?

Activity 7.5

During this home visit, what would you be looking for, what questions would you be asking and what do you need to know? Would you ask your questions to both parents together or individually? Why?

Comment

Part of the assessment process is the gathering of information from different sources, being curious, working collaboratively and constantly reviewing the information. The initial referral came from the health visitor, what did they say in comparison to what you observed and what the parents said. Here you are looking for consistency. The parents informed the health visitor that the puppies were being trained and they wanted them to 'grow' with the children. This was important for the family. Is this what the parents told you? Did you speak to both parents together or separately? Together they are likely to provide you with the same story, separately what do they tell you? Are they consistent with what they are telling you? This is an important factor in safeguarding children and what Dykes (2019) refers to as triangulation. Triangulation within this context refers to gathering information from different sources and identifying consistencies and inconsistences and thus trying to identify the facts. The health visitor expressed concerns about the puppies; however, there were no health concerns in relation to the children. The question you need to ask yourself is: are the children at risk of significant harm? A point to consider is whether the concerns about the puppies are real, whether the puppies pose a risk to the children or whether there are other factors that are being overshadowed by the narrative relating to the puppies? You observe the two children on the floor surrounded by toys, but you may not have observed them moving. Is this a serious concern? What you may have is child abuse, which has been overshadowed by the concerns regarding the puppies. What might be needed is a Section 47 enquiry.

Analysing information

You have gathered information from many different sources, and although this is an ongoing process, you need to think about writing the analysis section of the assessment.

Some description is required, for example the situation and circumstances. This needs to be short and succinct. You also need to include some contextual information, for example what is the purpose of the assessment and why are Children's Services involved. The analysis will comprise of synthesising the information gathered, which is not just about summarising, but rather combining and highlighting the significance of the information making reference to similarities, differences and consistencies or inconsistencies. This is where you need to apply your critical thinking and critical analysis skills (Dykes, 2019). First of all, the writing of the analysis section of any assessment must be in a language that is understandable: no jargon or acronyms. Secondly, it needs to be based on factual information and not opinion or hearsay.

Let's look at what we mean by critical thinking and critical analysis. Within social work we are referring to evaluating information, reviewing information, critiquing and examining information in greater detail. The information we are referring to is the information gathered through the assessment process. It is this information that now needs to be analysed and presented. The important aspects of critical thinking and critical analysis include:

- evaluating the information, weighing up the strengths and limitations, for example the factual against opinion or hearsay, making comparisons such as who said what and comparing what others said to identify consistencies and inconsistencies;
- looking at different perspectives, being objective, listening to and enabling all individuals to express their own perspectives and ensuring these are included within the analysis, their story, their words;
- reflecting on the assessment process, the referral, the purpose, the gathering of information, considering who was included and why, whose voice was included and why, whose voice was absent and why, self-examining in relation to being objective or subjective or did anyone influence your decision, was your decision based on facts; and
- looking deeper and exploring how your beliefs, values and if, and how, your emotions played a part, and questioning how these impact on your professional judgements and subsequent decisions.

The information gathered will inform the decision-making process. The assessment will present the child's, parent's and family's situation and circumstances in a non-biased, non-judgemental manner. The social worker will have taken into consideration what it is like living in that house through the eyes of the child, the child's journey to where they are today, their current situation and circumstances, their wishes and feelings and their voice.

Decision-making

Decision-making follows the analysis and is where evidence is presented in relation to what will happen next. This evidence might be presented in court, a child protection conference, or at a panel if requesting support. As you can see in Figure 7.1 – 'C', while gathering information, a decision might need to be made to support the family or protect the children. However, the gathering of information and analysis will continue. For instance, you refer the parents to a parenting programme and continue the assessment. The parent's attendance, participation and subsequent parenting will be included in the assessment. The team manager would have been included throughout the assessment process during informal and formal supervision sessions. Such discussions need to be recorded to evidence what was discussed and agreed. Throughout the assessment process, you would be working in partnership with the children and parents and the assessment would be shared with them. Killick and Taylor (2020) identify six stages to decision-making. They are:

Prepare as discussed previously; here you need to consider what the purpose of your involvement is and thoroughly prepare for all work to be undertaken.

Engage with all individuals who are relevant and appropriate.

Gather information from as many different sources as possible.

Analyse the information; identify the recommendations to be made.

Choose who you need to work with and who needs to be included within the assessment.

The assessment framework

The Assessment Framework (HM Government, 2020) provides a systemic way of recording, analysing and understanding what is happening to children within their families and the wider context of the community in which they live.

The Assessment Framework is illustrated in Figure 7.3 and includes three inter-related systems or domains, each of which has a number of sub-domains.

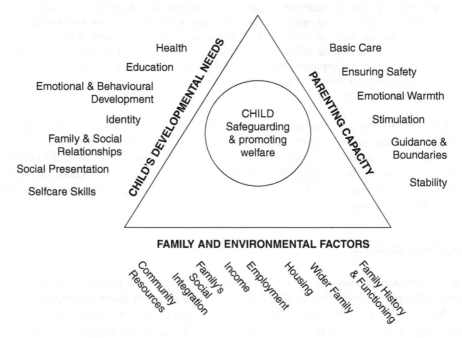

Figure 7.3 The Assessment Framework

(HM Government, 2020, p. 30)

The Assessment Framework is rooted in Child Development with an Emphasis on Child Developmental Needs, Parental Capacity and Wider Family and Environmental Factors. The social worker needs to have a thorough understanding of the child(ren) within the context of the child's family including their parents, extended family, and of the community and culture in which they are growing up.

Ecological framework and assessments

Within each of the three Domains, Figure 7.3, Child Developmental Needs, Parental Capacity and Family and Environmental Factors, we can identify the importance of, and interplay between, relationships. The home environment is where the children and parents, each with their own ecosystems, as discussed in Chapter 3, engage and interact with each other. Exploring these ecosystems can provide invaluable information about the immediate relationships within the home along with family functioning, other family members and the wider environment, such as community, school, employment in addition to the macrosystem which will influence and impact all family members directly and indirectly (Bronfenbrenner, 1979/2005). As a social worker, you will need to gain an understanding of the parent's microsystem, their relationships, internal and external to the family home, to identify whether there are sources of stress, anxiety or health-related issues that are impacting on their ability to parent. The family and wider environmental factors play a significant part in the assessment in identifying sources of support, such as wider family members. Each family member will have their own ecosystem, as discussed in Chapter 3, which you will need to explore. You can begin to see the importance of applying the ecological framework (PPCT) (Bronfenbrenner, 2005), discussed in Chapter 3, in your assessments. For instance:

Child's developmental needs (Figure 7.3)

Process – the developmental process. Child's Developmental Needs, see Figure 7.3, when you look at the sub-domains are the child's needs being met? Are the parent's able to provide the sub-domains relating to parental capacity? What influence/impact does the family and environmental factors have on the child's development?

Person – the biological, cognitive, emotional and behavioural characteristics of the individual. Child's Developmental Needs, see Figure 7.3: here we can see the importance of observations in relation to behaviour, self-care, social presentation and relationships along with questions about education and identity.

Context – the four nested systems: the microsystem, mesosystem, exosystem and macrosystem. Assessing a child's systems would include observations and explorative questions about their relationships within and external to the family home. This would include identifying what is influencing or impacting upon the child's development, their behaviour, their education. What is influencing their characteristics and identity formation?

Time – chronosystem; for example, historical time, parent–child time, family time, time with friends.

The ecological framework will enable you to explore historical information and family relationships. Additionally, this will provide invaluable information in relation to the parent's beliefs, attitudes, aspirations and their understanding of parenting and child developmental needs.

Habitus, capital and field and assessment

The conceptual tools of Bourdieu (1977, 1984, 1991), as discussed in Chapter 3, will facilitate the exploration of each individual's habitus, capital and field. Figure 7.4 provides an overview.

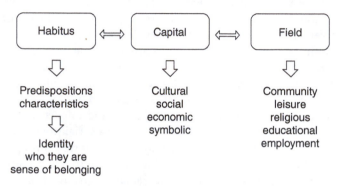

Figure 7.4   Habitus, capital and field

Habitus

You will be able to gain a greater understanding of the parent/child by exploring their habitus; their internalised predispositions, characteristics along with their values and beliefs. In addition, to how they act and engage in everyday life including the choices and the activities in which they participate can be explored and observed. For example, this information would provide invaluable information in relation to Parental Capacity, Figure 7.3, and how the parent was parented/socialised as a child and as a parent where their strengths are, what their needs are and what influences and impacts upon their world. The family home is predominantly where the child grows, develops and thus their habitus is formed. Children are socialised to the world around them, their parent's world, community and are introduced to the wider social, economic and political world through their parents, wider family members and friends. Here we can observe the intergenerational transmission of beliefs, values and many of their parent's perspectives.

Capitals

You could explore the parent's capitals, in relation to Parental Capacity, Child Developmental Needs and Family and Environmental Factors, Figure 7.3, through a variety of different approaches. Some tools to facilitate this exploration will be discussed later in this chapter but firstly let's revisit Activity 3.2 in Chapter 3. Here you made a note of the capitals you have. Reflecting on this activity, complete Activity 7.5.

Activity 7.6

Thinking about Parental Capacity, Child Developmental Needs and Family and Environmental Factors in relation to the four types of capitals, cultural capital, social capital, economic capital and symbolic capital, what questions would you ask a parent to identify their capitals?

You need to consider the phrasing and language of your questions, how you are going to clarify your understanding of what they have said, and how you are going to help them explore the relevancy and importance of capitals.

Comment

You could ask the parents about their education or about their previous caring responsibilities. Do they have extended family members or friends to draw upon for support. Maybe they are employed or own their home. What qualifications and employment do they have, or are they a member or lead a group? You need to acknowledge that everyone has capitals but they will to be different for different individuals. For example, a parent might not have any formal qualifications but has a thorough understanding of their child's needs because of their previous experiences.

Cultural capital

This is the parents' knowledge, skills and behaviour in relation to parenting. What is their understanding of those dimensions, see Figure 7.3: basic care, ensuring safety, emotional warmth, stimulation, guidance and boundaries and stability? What is their understanding of child developmental needs? Does their understanding impact on their ability to parent or their ability to change? Through explorative discussions these dimensions can be investigated. Any intervention, in partnership with the parents, could build and develop on their knowledge and skills through the development of their cultural capital, for example attendance at a parenting programme. The questions you might ask yourself are: what is the purpose of attending a parenting programme and how will I know if it has made a difference?

Social capital

This relates to the parents' social support networks such as family and friends in addition to community involvement and resources. Relationships could be explored to identify whether these were supportive or a form of stress and include frequency of contact. A parent's social capital could include attending a parent and toddler group and thus increase their social networks.

Economic capital

The Family and Environmental Factors of the Assessment Framework, in part, relates to economic capital, for example employment, income and housing. All three areas are potentially areas of security, safety and stress. Housing might, for example, be private rented, the parents might be unemployed and in receipt of welfare benefits. If there is uncertainty with the housing tenancy, or unemployment, which may lead to financial constraints and potentially stress, this could impact on their ability to parent. We need to remember that parental stress can be attributed to child abuse.

Symbolic capital

Symbolic capital (Bourdieu, 1991) relates to socially recognised and sanctioned prestige or honour. This could be in the form of education, employment or community status. Some parents have no formal educational qualifications, are unemployed and do not engage within their community; they have few resources and little support. Often these families are isolated, marginalised and many stigmatised. Working with parents, and working in partnership with them, you could explore how they could develop their symbolic capital through community engagement, education, employment or support groups.

Field

Bourdieu's (1977, 1991) field represents the social and institutional places and spaces or networks where the family may be socially positioned. Field includes social, cultural, educational, religious, artistic, economic or intellectual environments. Field could be the community, school or place of work. This will be different for each family, but could also be different for each family member. Their position within the field will also be different. Through explorative dialogue you could explore the various fields that family members occupy, their position within each field and whether a particular field is a source of support or stress. Field could also include technology and their positioning within various social media, gaming and employment hierarchies within these fields.

Habitus, capital and field

Each of these elements provide a greater understanding of the individual, whether a child or parent, and when considered with the Assessment Framework (HM Government, 2020), it gives an overall representation of, for example the child's development and their needs and the parent's strengths, needs and support networks. Assessment tools such as genograms, ecomaps and culturagrams could be used to facilitate such discussions. These will be discussed later in this chapter.

We will now explore the Assessment Framework (HM Government, 2020), through a Case Study 7.2 and Activity 7.7, see Figure 7.3.

Case study

Barbara and Sam are the parents of two children, Becky, aged 6, and Joseph, aged 10. Barbara works part-time in the local shop, while Sam works shifts at a local factory. There is uncertainty about Sam's continuation of employment. This has created stress in their relationship which has included some arguments. The children have heard some of these arguments which have included some during the night. This has resulted in them waking up and being distressed. On some occasions, Barbara has taken the children and stayed at her parent's house. This has resulted in them not attending school. During these occasions Sam has started drinking which has exacerbated the situation. Barbara's parents have been supportive and offered to assist with their finances, but Sam is not happy about this. School has made a referral to Children's Services because when Joseph arrived at school, following a four-day absence for being ill, he had several bruises to one of his legs and arms. Joseph told the teachers that he had fallen off his bike.

Activity 7.7

Thinking about the Case Study above, you are undertaking an assessment. Consideration needs to be given to Figure 7.3 – the three domains and sub-domains, to identify whether Joseph has suffered significant harm or is at risk of suffering significant harm. Additionally, you are undertaking an assessment to identify whether Becky is at risk of suffering significant harm.

Using Bronfenbrenner's (2005) ecological framework, what questions would you ask the parents, and the children, about their relationships with each other, with their grandparents and with the wider community?

Using the conceptual tools of Bourdieu (1977, 1984, 1991), habitus, capital and field, what questions would you ask the parents, and the children, to explore the children's habitus, capital and field?

Comment

Within the assessment we would identify the relationships within the family home such as the parent's relationship, and each parent and each child, and the children's relationship with each other. There are also relationships with each individual within the family home and Barbara's parents. There are also relationships with Barbara and her employer, Sam and her employer and the children and their schools. There are also relationships between the family and the community.

Through explorative questions you will gain an understanding of Barbara and Sam's microsystems; their relationships, internal and external to the family home. Here you will identify whether there are sources of stress, anxiety or health-related issues that are impacting on the family. For example, Sam's anxiety about the possibility of becoming unemployed. This is having a direct impact on Barbara and an indirect impact on the children resulting in them waking in the night distressed in addition to missing school.

Within each of the three domains and sub-domains, Child Developmental Needs, Parental Capacity and Family and Environmental Factors, we can identify the risk factors and protective factors.

A risk factor is Sam – employment concerns, drinking and the potential of domestic abuse. This is having an impact on both Barbara and Sam's ability to parent. The children's development, health and well-being are at risk because of the potential domestic abuse and Sam's drinking.

A protective factor is Barbara's parents who have provided her and the children with support and the offer of financial support.

Drawing on the conceptual tools of Bourdieu (1977, 1984), as discussed in Chapter 3, a greater understanding of the lives of Barbara, Sam, Joseph and Becky can be gained, individually and as a family. You could explore each individual's habitus, capital and field to develop your understanding of their strengths, needs and risks.

Habitus

You will be able to gain a greater understanding of Barbara, Sam, Joseph and Becky by exploring their habitus. Here questions to Barbara and Sam could be about their childhood, siblings, parents and wider family members in addition to education. Questions for Joseph and Becky could include what they like doing at home, when they go out and where they go. Questions could include school, engagement in the community. When asking questions to Joseph and Becky you need to consider language, the environment where you are meeting them and consideration given to confidentiality, for example home, school, grandparents and whether you are alone. You might consider creating an activity for them to tell you about them; consider including questions about their favourite colour, food and what they like doing. For their engagement make it interactive and fun.

Capitals

Revisiting Activity 7.5, and the questions you created to explore the parent's capitals.

Could these be used or adapted, to explore Barbara and Sam's cultural capital, social capital, economic capital and symbolic capital? Questions might include talking to them about their education, their children's needs, family and friends, community engagement and employment.

Field

This would include exploring the various fields such as the family home, school, community and employer. There is some anxiety for Sam in relation to employment and this has the potential to impact on her and the family's, economic capital.

Assessment

Joseph has informed the teacher that he fell off his bike, this accident occurred when he was out with his mother and grandparents. You could explore this further through discussions with Joseph, Barbara and his grandparents. This is what Dykes (2019) refers to as triangulation as discussed previously. Sam's anxiety could be explored and raising her awareness to the impact of the arguments on the children and Barbara could alleviate this situation. You could explore the time element, chronosystem (Bronfenbrenner, 2005), in relation to the arguments, individually and together, with Sam and Barbara. For example, are these arguments a cause of the stress associated with the anxiety of employment uncertainties. Or, have these arguments, and the potential of domestic abuse, occurred over a longer time period. Assessment tools such as genograms, ecomaps and culturagrams could be used to facilitate such discussions.

Assessment tools

Genograms

Genograms are invaluable when exploring family composition (Dykes, 2019; Parker, 2021). They are similar to a family tree in that they provide a visual representation of family members and their relationships (Killick and Taylor, 2020). Genograms are created in partnership with the family. The creation of the genogram can therefore provide an opportunity to build a relationship with the family along with identifying support networks and potential forms of stress. Genograms can be used to explore the various forms of capital a parent may have, which in turn could identify strengths, needs and potential risks. There are a number of symbols used in the creation of a genogram (Dykes, 2019; Killick and Taylor, 2020; Parker, 2021) and the most common being (Figures 7.5 and 7.6):

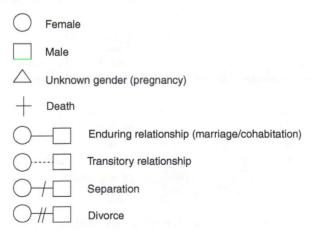

Figure 7.5 Genogram symbols

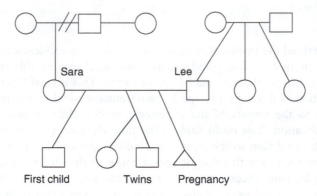

Figure 7.6 Genogram example

Exploring family relationships

As we see in the example above, the family consists of Sara (mother), Lee (father) and their three children. Sara is pregnant.

Sara

Sara was the only child to her parents who are divorced. Exploring Sara's relationship with her parents would enable you to gain an understanding of the impact of the divorce. Here we could consider how the divorce impacted upon Sara's habitus, for example her confidence, self-esteem, identity and her relationships with family and friends. Exploring Sara's relationship with Lee would provide a greater understanding of their relationship. This understanding is significant in the assessment of parenting capacity, meeting the children's needs and identifying the strengths, needs and risks of the family. Within the exploration of Sara's relationship with her parents we could begin to build a picture of her habitus: the predispositions and characteristics that contribute towards who Sara is. This would include her identity and her sense of belonging, as a child, within her family, wider family, friends and community. You could expand on this information further by exploring the impact of her parent's divorce. This would be further developed to include when Sara met Lee and their relationship. Here you would be gaining an understanding of Sara's identity and sense of belonging within her own family. Sara's capital could be explored to identify Sara's knowledge and understanding of her children's need, support networks and her social integration in the wider community. This would identify the various fields that she visits, attends and participates in. What you are doing is building a picture of Sara's life, past and present. Consideration should also be given to her aspirations and where she sees herself in the future.

Lee

We can see that Lee's parents are married or cohabiting and are in a long-term relationship. Lee has two sisters. That Lee is positioned on the left-hand side would indicate that he is the eldest. You would undertake the same explorative discussions with Lee, as you did with Sara, to gain an understanding of his habitus, a greater understanding of his capitals and the fields that he visits, attends and participates in. An example of such might include identifying that Lee remains in contact with some friends from college, but has recently been made redundant and is pursuing other employment opportunities.

The family

Sara and Lee have a son, twins, one girl and one boy, and Sara is pregnant. You would add names, ages and dates of birth of the children to the genogram. Establishing the various relationships between Sara and Lee, along with exploring their capitals, individually and together, would enable you to build up a picture of the family. This would include strengths – protective factors, needs – support networks, and stressors – risk factors. This could be further developed through the creation of an ecomap.

Ecomaps

Ecomaps are another very useful tool (Dykes, 2019; Killick and Taylor, 2020; Parker, 2021). These can visually illustrate family networks along with identifying connections between individuals, environments and institutions. Here, we can observe and identify the interconnectivity between the various relationships. Additionally, there is the opportunity to explore both the individuals' and family's capitals (Bourdieu, 1977, 1984). Again, these would be completed with the family. Figure 7.7 is an example of an ecomap for Sara and Lee.

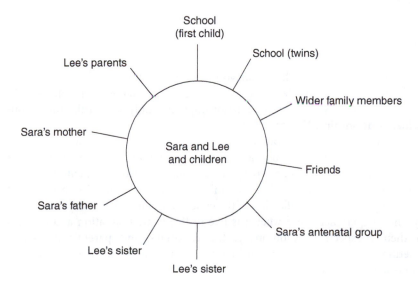

Figure 7.7 Example of an ecomap

Culturagrams

Genograms and ecomaps are an invaluable tool for identifying family composition and support networks. Another one is the culturagram. As highlighted in Chapters 1 and 2, in addition to the PCF, KSS and the professional standards, you should be aware, recognise and acknowledge cultural diversity. Therefore, when undertaking assessments with individuals from different ethnicities, you need to understand their culture. Culture should not be viewed as a single perspective but rather multidimensional. The culturagram will enable you to gain a greater understanding of the family and each family member. Congress (1994) suggests the following areas should be considered when creating a culturagram:

- reasons for immigration,
- length of time in the community,
- legal or undocumented status,
- age at time of immigration,
- language spoken at home and in the community,
- contact with cultural institutions,
- health beliefs,
- holidays and special events,
- impact of crisis events,
- values about family, education, and work.

(Congress, 1994, p. 2)

You can apply a flexible approach when completing a culturagram as some areas will not be relevant. However, they do provide an overview of the areas to explore to develop your understanding about the family, the individual members of the family, their identity, lived experiences, their stories, journey, status, beliefs, values and community connections.

Tools

Tools such as those above will provide you with opportunities to develop your skills and learn about individuals and families and build trust and develop relationships. This will enable you to identify and explore relationships, not only within the same household, but wider relationships. You might also include, for example Lee and his sisters or Sara and Lee's sisters. This again provides valuable information in relation to support or tension, anxiety or relief. The use of such tools can help you in a manner that respects the individual. This includes practising in a culturally sensitive and culturally responsive way. This not only includes cultural humility, but also individual humility. Such tools could assist you in the identification of the child's and parent's journey to where they are today, their experiences, and what it is like to live in that situation and circumstances from their perspective. Additionally, the children's and parent's participation in completing genograms, ecomaps and culturagrams enables them to contribute to the decision-making process.

Foundations of professional social work practice

When we look at the assessment process, we can see that all of the areas that we discussed, explored and examined throughout the chapters are included within Figure 7.5 foundations of professional social work practice. We presented the foundations of professional social work practice in Chapter 1, Figure 1.5 and Chapter 2, Figure 2.2. This includes professionalism and the way social workers present themselves, their practice is underpinned by theory and their knowledge is continually developing through study, experience and critical reflection. The social worker is conscious of their values and how these might impact on the manner in which they work with individuals. Their practice is ethical, promoting equality, challenging oppression and discrimination, and empowering individuals. You can begin to see the interconnectivity between all of the components in Figure 7.8 and how theories such as Bronfenbrenner and Bourdieu can underpin practice in addition to the application of other theories, models, approaches and perspectives to facilitate social work practice including safeguarding and assessment. Here you can see how these aspects align with the PCF, Professional Standards and KSS. You can also see the importance of becoming a reflexive social worker and critically questioning your own beliefs, values and assumptions and the potential impact of these on other individuals and of building relationships.

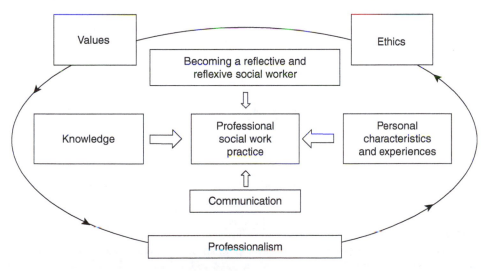

Figure 7.8 Professional social work practice

Chapter summary

This chapter began by introducing you to assessments. You developed your under-standing of the PCF Super Domains of Purpose, Practice, Impact. This included developing your knowledge of the assessment as a process. During the assessment process, you recognised the importance of supervision for support but also to ensure accountability and that policies and procedures are being followed and you are working within the legislative framework. You looked at the significance of building a compre-hensive understanding of the family and the child's world. You have developed your knowledge and understanding of the skills required to undertake assessments, such as the importance of communication skills including questioning self and others. You developed your understanding of the Assessment Framework (HM Government, 2020) and application of the ecological framework (Bronfenbrenner) and the conceptual tools of Bourdieu: habitus, capital and field, within the assessment process. In the final section of this chapter, you have learned about some of the tools that are available to facilitate explorative discussions with families. These tools can enable you to explore family life, the interconnectedness of systems and individual capitals.

Further reading

Diaz, C (2020) *Decision Making in Child and Family Social Work Perspectives on Children's Participation*. Bristol: Policy Press.

This book focuses on children and parent's participation in decision-making. The book explores why participation is important, theoretical concepts of participation and the concept of good social work practice including evidence-based practice. The book is based on the author's research and provides insight into the views and perceptions of young people and professionals involved in key decision-making forums namely child protection conferences and child in care reviews.

Dykes, C (2019) *Writing Analytical Assessments in Social Work*, 2nd edn. St Albans: Critical Publishing.

This book offers a critical discussion about the assessment process. Assessment tools such as genograms and ecomaps are explored through practical examples. There is a comprehensive discussion on writing assessments and developing knowledge, understanding and skills in analysis and presenting the facts.

Killick, C and Taylor, B (2020) *Assessment, Risk and Decision Making in Social Work: An Introduction*. London: Sage/Learning Matters.

This comprehensive introductory book provides an examination of the assessment and decision-making process. The book provides an overview and defines key terms, explores specialist aspects of assessments and decision-making. Developing professional skills, making professional judgements and legal and ethical aspects of assessments along with using assessment tools are also included.

Conclusion

The content of this book is designed to meet the core elements of the requirements for social work education. The book has been primarily written for social work students who are starting their journey to becoming a social worker, in addition to developing their skills and understanding of the requirements for practice. The book also set out to meet the Social Work Subject Benchmark Statements (Quality Assurance Agency (QAA), 2019). These include understanding the nature of social work and developing knowledge and understanding under the following headings:

- Social work services and service users
- Values and ethics
- Social work theory
- The nature of social work practice.

Furthermore, this book aimed to enable you to meet the requirements of the Professional Capabilities Framework (PCF) (BASW, 2018). This book will have given you a good introductory understanding of children and family social work practice.

Book structure

Through an interactive approach with figures, activities, case studies and research summaries, this book set out to support your reflection, in addition to evaluating and reviewing your learning and development. The chapters will have developed your knowledge and understanding of working with children and families. Additionally, there has been a focus on skills development, for example questioning, communication and observation skills. Within the chapters you have been encouraged to start to examine your own values, views and perspectives and to think about the origins of these. Each of the seven chapters has concentrated on a different aspect of social work in relation to working with children and families.

In Chapter 1, we laid the foundations of your journey to becoming a social worker through the exploration of the concepts of profession, professional and professionalism within the context of social work. You also considered the Knowledge and Skills Statement for the Child and Family Practitioner and the UK's four Social Work Professional Body's Professional Standards. Following these initial explorations, emphasis was placed on preparing for social work practice and included communication skills, recognising that social work is multidisciplinary and the importance of gaining knowledge and understanding of different subject areas. Finally, the chapter introduced you to critical reflection and of the significance of becoming a reflexive social worker.

Chapter 2 examined what is meant by social work values and ethics. You explored where we get our values from and how values might influence our relationships with other people. You also considered whether your values inform the decisions that you make. Following our exploration of values, you explored what is meant by ethics. Building on your understanding of values and ethics, you looked at the ladder of inference. This was illustrated as a tool to explore beliefs, assumptions and how actions can be based on those beliefs and assumptions. A research summary was introduced for you to consider values, ethics, beliefs and assumptions in addition to the potential impact of labelling individuals. The focus then switched to exploring cultural awareness, cultural competence and cultural humility. The chapter closed by exploring communicative ethics, narrative ethics, and values and ethics in the digital world.

Chapter 3 concentrated on an introduction to the theoretical constructs of Bronfenbrenner's (1979, 2005) ecological framework and Bourdieu's (1977, 1984, 1991, 2003) concepts of habitus, capital and field. You explored these constructs in relation to social work practice with a focus on working with children and families. You developed your knowledge gained in Chapter 1 relating to becoming a critically reflexive social worker in addition to considering Bronfenbrenner and Bourdieu's theoretical constructs. The chapter closed through examining the implications of applying such theories to practice.

In Chapter 4, the focus was on exploring what we mean by family. You explored the 'traditional' family along with contemporary families. You were invited to consider your perspectives of what 'family' means and from where these perspectives might originate. You explored how families are represented within policies. Here you built on your knowledge gained in the previous chapters relating to communication and in particular language, in addition to labelling, and examining how different representations of individuals might be oppressive rather than supportive. You then explored the crucial issue of invisibility and how some families become invisible, but visible by the nature of the label that is attached to them. The chapter closed by exploring how we might describe family practices and how we display ourselves as a family.

In Chapter 5, we focused on working with children and young people. Reference was made to the coronavirus pandemic (COVID-19) 2020–2021, where you considered the potential impact on children. The emphasis of this chapter was on working with children and young people and through a series of scenarios, and using the dramaturgical model of reflection introduced in Chapter 1, you considered how you might prepare to work with children and young people.

In Chapter 6, you explored what is meant by safeguarding. This included exploring what is meant by harm, risk and abuse. Reference was made to the Children Act 1989 and the Working Together to Safeguard Children: A Guide to Inter-Agency Working to Safeguard and Promote the Welfare of Children (HM Government, 2020). You focused on developing your understanding of abuse through exploration of the four categories identified within the guidance. Through a case study you explored whether a situation was a safeguarding issue. You examined the initial reason for social work involvement, but more importantly gained an understanding of the significance of your observations and questioning. You considered an activity, which asked whether another situation was a safeguarding issue. Both the case study and the activity enabled you to consider safeguarding from different perspectives.

The final chapter focused on the assessment process. You considered the PCF Super Domains and the importance of having a thorough understanding of the purpose of your involvement. You then considered aspects of your practice and finally the impact this has made. You explored the components of the assessment process developing your understanding of multi-agency working and information sharing. You developed your skills for gathering information building on the knowledge gained in the previous chapters and exploring communication and observations. You looked at analysing information and how this important aspect informs your decision-making. You explored the Assessment Framework and made links to the theories discussed in Chapter 3. Some assessment tools that assist in the gathering of information were explored. Throughout the chapters you considered the PCF along with the Super Domains in addition to the KSS and the Professional Standards.

Professional development

In Chapter 1, we observed that Jordan (1984) invites us to the 'academic discipline' (p. 1) of social work. He acknowledges that social work is not the same as many other academic disciplines, but a practical activity that requires personal qualities that are as important as the knowledge they possess. These personal qualities include communication – verbal and non-verbal and how you conduct and present yourself. This book has emphasised the importance of developing, and building on, the skills associated with such qualities. In addition to developing the knowledge and skills required for children and families social work, you have explored the importance of preparing for practice. This has included considering the PCF Super Domains.

Purpose: Why we do what we do as social workers, our values and ethics, and how we approach our work.

Practice: What we do – the specific skills, knowledge, interventions and critical analytic abilities we develop to act and do social work.

Impact: How we make a difference and how we know we make a difference. Our ability to bring about change through our practice, through our leadership, through understanding our context and through our overall professionalism.

(BASW, 2018)

During your social work training and throughout your career you need to consider your professional development, including those personal qualities (Jordan, 1984), your knowledge and understanding of children and families social work, your skills and examining your values. In order to develop these aspects, reflection is essential.

You need to become a reflexive social worker and through self-questioning continually evaluate your practice. The dramaturgical approach of reflection will enable you to reflect on your practice in addition to preparing for practice.

Three questions

In Chapter 1, three questions were asked: Does social work work? What should a social worker be able to do? What should a social worker know? (Timms and Timms, 1977).

What should a social worker know can be answered through examining the Knowledge and Skills Statement for Child and Family Practitioners, in addition to the PCF and the Professional Standards. What should a social worker be able to do, again, is illustrated through the Knowledge and Skills Statement, PCF and Professional Standards in addition to those personal qualities that facilitate the development, building and maintaining of relationships. The question – does social work work – might not be so easy to answer, and here we would refer to evidence-based practice. This question is one that you may wish to return to throughout your studies, and throughout your professional career. I would like to invite you to answer the question yourself.

Activity 8.1

Visit the NSPCC website where you will find a list of the serious case reviews, significant case reviews or multi-agency child practice reviews. Upon reading a selection of these revisit the question – does social work work?

Visit the Gov.UK website and look for the Evaluation and Summary Reports for the Children's Social Care Innovation Programme (CSCIP). Upon reading a selection of these reports revisit the question – does social work work?

Visit the What Works for Children's Social Care website and read a selection of research reports and revisit the question – does social work work?

When on placement, and when you become a qualified social worker, consider the PCF Super Domain, Impact, how do you know that your practice has made a difference? Have you evaluated your practice?

Comment

Through reading the above reports you are developing your critical analysis skills in addition to increasing your knowledge and understanding of social work practice. This is part of your continuing professional development.

Key themes

Throughout the chapters we have identified a number of key themes that are very important with social work and working with children and families. These include the importance of professionalism. This includes presentation of self, continuing professional development, working in partnership with children, parents, families and other professionals. Communication skills are essential within all aspects of working with individuals. We also identified how important our values are to working with individuals along with practicing ethically. Ethical practice includes being open and honest, respecting diversity, questioning and challenging our own beliefs and assumptions. Here we need to also consider challenging oppression, discrimination, labelling and stereo-typing individually and structurally. As social workers we need to ensure our practice is underpinned by theories, research and that we are working within the legislative framework. Here again, we can make links to ethical practice and ensuring all of our decisions are based on sound professional judgements and factual evidence. This demonstrates the importance of recognising and observing the interconnectivity between individuals and between individuals and environments and the impact thereof on their growth, development, and health and well-being. The conceptual tools of habitus, capitals and field are significant in the identification of assessing individual's predispositions and characteristics, knowledge and understanding, social networks and economic well-being. Identifying the interconnectivity between relationships along exploring habitus, capital and field in social work practice provides an invaluable opportunity for exploring and gaining an understanding of all aspects of children's, young people's and parent's lives including stressors, strengths, needs and risks. They also provide the opportunity to identify inequality, marginalisation and stigmatisation and the subsequent impact on children and families. Additionally, as social workers we need to be aware of what is happening locally, nationally and internationally, for example COVID-19 and the impact of such on all individuals. As your journey through your social course comes to an end, your journey as a newly qualified social worker will begin. Here you will undertake your Assessed and Supported Year in Employment (ASYE). Remember, your learning and development never ends, your journey of dis-covery, self, other people, knowledge and understanding needs to remain as your pro-fessional growth, learning and development continues as you progress in your career.

Useful websites

NSPCC: Serious Case Reviews. https://learning.nspcc.org.uk/case-reviews.

Gov.UK: Evaluation and Summary Reports for the Children's Social Care Innovation Programme. https://www.gov.uk/guidance/childrens-social-care-innovation-programme-insights-and-evaluation.

What Works for Children's Social Care: https://whatworks-csc.org.uk/.

Appendix 1

Professional capabilities framework

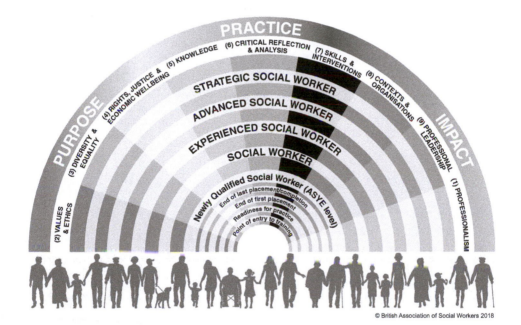

© British Association of Social Workers 2018

The nine domains

1. PROFESSIONALISM – Identify and behave as a professional social worker, committed to professional development.
2. VALUES AND ETHICS – Apply social work ethical principles and value to guide professional practices.
3. DIVERSITY AND EQUALITY – Recognise diversity and apply anti-discriminatory and anti-oppressive principles in practice.
4. RIGHTS, JUSTICE AND ECONOMIC WELL-BEING – Advance human rights and promote social justice and economic well-being.
5. KNOWLEDGE – Develop and apply relevant knowledge from social work practice and research, social sciences, law, other professional and relevant fields, and from the experience of people who use services.

6. CRITICAL REFLECTION AND ANALYSIS – Apply critical reflection and analysis to inform and provide a rationale for professional decision-making.
7. SKILLS AND INTERVENTIONS – Use judgement, knowledge and authority to intervene with individuals, families and communities to promote independence, provide support, prevent harm and enable progress.
8. CONTEXTS AND ORGANISATIONS – Engage with, inform, and adapt to changing organisational contexts, and the social and policy environments that shape practice. Operate effectively within and contribute to the development of organisations and services, including multi-agency and inter-professional settings.
9. PROFESSIONAL LEADERSHIP – Promote the profession and good social work practice. Take responsibility for the professional learning and development of others. Develop personal influence and be part of the collective leadership and impact of the profession.

Published with kind permission of BASW – www.basw.co.uk.

Appendix 2

Subject benchmark for social work

5 Knowledge, understanding and skills

Subject knowledge and understanding

5.1 During their qualifying degree studies in social work, students acquire, critically evaluate, apply and integrate knowledge and understanding in the following five core areas of study.

5.2 Social work theory, which includes:

i. critical explanations from social work theory and other subjects which contribute to the knowledge base of social work

ii. an understanding of social work's rich and contested history from both a UK and comparative perspective

iii. the relevance of sociological and applied psychological perspectives to understanding societal and structural influences on human behaviour at individual, group and community levels, and the relevance of sociological theorisation to a deeper understanding of adaptation and change

iv. the relevance of psychological, physical and physiological perspectives to understanding human, personal and social development, well-being and risk

v. social science theories explaining and exploring group and organisational behaviour

vi. the range of theories and research-informed evidence that informs understanding of the child, adult, family or community and of the range of assessment and interventions which can be used

vii. the theory, models and methods of assessment, factors underpinning the selection and testing of relevant information, knowledge and critical appraisal of relevant social science and other research and evaluation methodologies, and the evidence base for social work

viii. the nature of analysis and professional judgement and the processes of risk assessment and decision-making, including the theory of risk-informed decisions and the balance of choice and control, rights and protection in decision-making

ix. approaches, methods and theories of intervention in working with a diverse population within a wide range of settings, including factors guiding the choice and critical evaluation of these, and user-led perspectives.

5.3 Values and ethics, which include:

i. the nature, historical evolution, political context and application of professional social work values, informed by national and international definitions and ethical statements, and their relation to personal values, identities, influences and ideologies

ii. the ethical concepts of rights, responsibility, freedom, authority and power inherent in the practice of social workers as agents with statutory powers in different situations

iii. aspects of philosophical ethics relevant to the understanding and resolution of value dilemmas and conflicts in both interpersonal and professional context

iv. understanding of, and adherence to, the ethical foundations of empirical and conceptual research, as both consumers and producers of social science research

v. the relationship between human rights enshrined in law and the moral and ethical rights determined theoretically, philosophically and by contemporary society

vi. the complex relationships between justice, care and control in social welfare and the practical and ethical implications of these, including their expression in roles as statutory agents in diverse practice settings and in upholding the law in respect of challenging discrimination and inequalities

vii. the conceptual links between codes defining ethical practice and the regulation of professional conduct

viii. the professional and ethical management of potential conflicts generated by codes of practice held by different professional groups

ix. the ethical management of professional dilemmas and conflicts in balancing the perspectives of individuals who need care and support and professional decision-making at points of risk, care and protection

x. the constructive challenging of individuals and organisations where there may be conflicts with social work values, ethics and codes of practice

xi. the professional responsibility to be open and honest if things go wrong (the duty of candour about own practice) and to act on concerns about poor or unlawful practice by any person or organisation

xii. continuous professional development as a reflective, informed and skilled practitioner, including the constructive use of professional supervision.

5.4 Service users and carers, which include:

i. the factors which contribute to the health and well-being of individuals, families and communities, including promoting dignity, choice and independence for people who need care and support

ii. the underpinning perspectives that determine explanations of the characteristics and circumstances of people who need care and support, with critical evaluation drawing on research, practice experience and the experience and expertise of people who use services

iii. the social and psychological processes associated with, for example, poverty, migration, unemployment, trauma, poor health, disability, lack of education and other sources of disadvantage and how they affect well-being, how they interact and may lead to marginalisation, isolation and exclusion, and demand for social work services

iv. explanations of the links between the factors contributing to social differences and identities (for example, social class, gender, ethnic differences, age, sexuality and religious belief) and the structural consequences of inequality and differential need faced by service users

v. the nature and function of social work in a diverse and increasingly global society (with particular reference to prejudice, interpersonal relations, discrimination, empowerment and anti-discriminatory practices).

5.5 The nature of social work practice, in the UK and more widely, which includes:

i. the place of theoretical perspectives and evidence from European and international research in assessment and decision-making processes

ii. the integration of theoretical perspectives and evidence from European and international research into the design and implementation of effective social work intervention with a wide range of service users, carers and communities

iii. the knowledge and skills which underpin effective practice, with a range of service users and in a variety of settings

iv. the processes that facilitate and support service user and citizen rights, choice, co-production, self-governance, well-being and independence

v. the importance of interventions that promote social justice, human rights, social cohesion, collective responsibility and respect for diversity and that tackle inequalities

vi. its delivery in a range of community-based and organisational settings spanning the statutory, voluntary and private sectors, and the changing nature of these service contexts

vii. the factors and processes that facilitate effective interdisciplinary, interprofessional and interagency collaboration and partnership across a plurality of settings and disciplines

viii. the importance of social work's contribution to intervention across service user groups, settings and levels in terms of the profession's focus on social justice, human rights, social cohesion, collective responsibility and respect for diversities

ix. the processes of reflection and reflexivity as well as approaches for evaluating service and welfare outcomes for vulnerable people, and their significance for the development of practice and the practitioner.

5.6 The leadership, organisation and delivery of social work services, which includes:

i. the location of contemporary social work within historical, comparative and global perspectives, including in the devolved nations of the UK and wider European and international contexts

ii. how the service delivery context is portrayed to service users, carers, families and communities

iii. the changing demography and cultures of communities, including European and international contexts, in which social workers practise

iv. the complex relationships between public, private, social and political philosophies, policies and priorities and the organisation and practice of social work, including the contested nature of these

v. the issues and trends in modern public and social policy and their relationship to contemporary practice, service delivery and leadership in social work

vi. the significance of legislative and legal frameworks and service delivery standards, including on core social work values and ethics in the delivery of services which support, enable and empower

vii. the current range and appropriateness of statutory, voluntary and private agencies providing services and the organisational systems inherent within these

viii. development of new ways of working and delivery, for example the development of social enterprises, integrated multi-professional teams and independent social work provision

ix. the significance of professional and organisational relationships with other related services, including housing, health, education, police, employment, fire, income maintenance and criminal justice

x. the importance and complexities of the way agencies work together to provide care, the relationships between agency policies, legal requirements and professional boundaries in shaping the nature of services provided in integrated and interdisciplinary contexts

xi. the contribution of different approaches to management and leadership within different settings, and the impact on professional practice and on quality of care management and leadership in public and human services

xii. the development of person-centred services, personalised care, individual budgets and direct payments all focusing upon the human and legal rights of the service user for control, power and self-determination

xiii. the implications of modern information and communications technology for both the provision and receipt of services, use of technologically enabled support and the use of social media as a process and forum for vulnerable people, families and communities, and communities of professional practice.

Subject-specific skills and other skills

5.7 The range of skills required by a qualified social worker reflects the complex and demanding context in which they work. Many of these skills may be of value in many situations, for example, analytical thinking, building relationships, working as a member of an organisation, intervention, evaluation and reflection. What defines the specific nature of these skills as developed by social work students is:

i. the context in which they are applied and assessed (for example, communication skills in practice with people with sensory impairments or assessment skills in an interprofessional setting)

ii. the relative weighting given to such skills within social work practice (for example, the central importance of problem-solving skills within complex human situations)

iii. the specific purpose of skill development (for example, the acquisition of research skills in order to build a repertoire of research-based practice)

iv. a requirement to integrate a range of skills (that is, not simply to demonstrate these in an isolated and incremental manner).

5.8 All social work graduates demonstrate the ability to reflect on and learn from the exercise of their skills, in order to build their professional identity. They understand the significance of the concepts of continuing professional development and lifelong learning, and accept responsibility for their own continuing development.

5.9 Social work students acquire and integrate skills in the following five core areas.

Problem-solving skills

5.10   These are subdivided into four areas.

5.11   Managing problem-solving activities: graduates in social work are able to:

   i.   think logically, systematically, creatively, critically and reflectively, in order to carry out a holistic assessment

   ii.   apply ethical principles and practices critically in planning problem-solving activities

   iii.   plan a sequence of actions to achieve specified objectives, making use of research, theory and other forms of evidence

   iv.   manage processes of change, drawing on research, theory and other forms of evidence.

5.12   Gathering information: graduates in social work are able to:

   i.   demonstrate persistence in gathering information from a wide range of sources and using a variety of methods, for a range of purposes. These methods include electronic searches, reviews of relevant literature, policy and procedures, face-to-face interviews, and written and telephone contact with individuals and groups

   ii.   take into account differences of viewpoint in gathering information and critically assess the reliability and relevance of the information gathered

   iii.   assimilate and disseminate relevant information in reports and case records.

5.13   Analysis and synthesis: graduates in social work are able to analyse and synthesise knowledge gathered for problem-solving purposes, in order to:

   i.   assess human situations, taking into account a variety of factors (including the views of participants, theoretical concepts, research evidence, legislation and organisational policies and procedures)

   ii.   analyse and synthesise information gathered, weighing competing evidence and modifying their viewpoint in the light of new information, then relate this information to a particular task, situation or problem

   iii.   balance specific factors relevant to social work practice (such as risk, rights, cultural differences and language needs and preferences, responsibilities to protect vulnerable Individuals and legal obligations)

   iv.   assess the merits of contrasting theories, explanations, research, policies and procedures and use the information to develop and sustain reasoned arguments

   v.   employ a critical understanding of factors that support or inhibit problem-solving, including societal, organisational and community issues as well as individual relationships

   vi.   critically analyse and take account of the impact of inequality and discrimination in working with people who use social work services.

5.14   Intervention and evaluation: graduates in social work are able to use their knowledge of a range of interventions and evaluation processes creatively and selectively to:

   i.   build and sustain purposeful relationships with people and organisations in communities and interprofessional contexts

ii. make decisions based on evidence, set goals and construct specific plans to achieve outcomes, taking into account relevant information, including ethical guidelines

iii. negotiate goals and plans with others, analysing and addressing in a creative and flexible manner individual, cultural and structural impediments to change

iv. implement plans through a variety of systematic processes that include working in partnership

v. practice in a manner that promotes well-being, protects safety and resolves conflict

vi. act as a navigator, advocate and support to assist people who need care and support to take decisions and access services

vii. manage the complex dynamics of dependency and, in some settings, provide direct care and personal support to assist people in their everyday lives

viii. meet deadlines and comply with external requirements of a task

ix. plan, implement and critically monitor and review processes and outcomes

x. bring work to an effective conclusion, taking into account the implications for all involved

xi. use and evaluate methods of intervention critically and reflectively.

Communication skills

5.15 Graduates in social work are able to communicate clearly, sensitively and effectively (using appropriate methods which may include working with interpreters) with individuals and groups of different ages and abilities in a range of formal and informal situations, in order to:

i. engage individuals and organisations, who may be unwilling, by verbal, paper-based and electronic means to achieve a range of objectives, including changing behaviour

ii. use verbal and non-verbal cues to guide and inform conversations and interpretation of information

iii. negotiate and, where necessary, redefine the purpose of interactions with individuals and organisations and the boundaries of their involvement

iv. listen actively and empathetically to others, taking into account their specific needs and life experiences

v. engage appropriately with the life experiences of service users, to understand accurately their viewpoint, overcome personal prejudices and respond appropriately to a range of complex personal and interpersonal situations

vi. make evidence-informed arguments drawing from theory, research and practice wisdom, including the viewpoints of service users and/or others

vii. write accurately and clearly in styles adapted to the audience, purpose and context of the communication

viii. use advocacy skills to promote others' rights, interests and needs

ix. present conclusions verbally and on paper, in a structured form, appropriate to the audience for which these have been prepared

x. make effective preparation for, and lead, meetings in a productive way.

Skills in working with others

5.16   Graduates in social work are able to build relationships and work effectively with others, in order to:

    i.   involve users of social work services in ways that increase their resources, capacity and power to influence factors affecting their lives

    ii.   engage service users and carers and wider community networks in active consultation

    iii.   respect and manage differences such as organisational and professional boundaries and differences of identity and/or language

    iv.   develop effective helping relationships and partnerships that facilitate change for individuals, groups and organisations while maintaining appropriate personal and professional boundaries

    v.   demonstrate interpersonal skills and emotional intelligence that creates and develops relationships based on openness, transparency and empathy

    vi.   increase social justice by identifying and responding to prejudice, institutional discrimination and structural inequality

    vii.   operate within a framework of multiple accountability (for example, to agencies, the public, service users, carers and others)

    viii.   observe the limits of professional and organisational responsibility, using supervision appropriately and referring to others when required

    ix.   provide reasoned, informed arguments to challenge others as necessary, in ways that are most likely to produce positive outcomes.

Skills in personal and professional development

5.17   Graduates in social work are able to:

    i.   work at all times in accordance with codes of professional conduct and ethics

    ii.   advance their own learning and understanding with a degree of independence and use supervision as a tool to aid professional development

    iii.   develop their professional identity, recognise their own professional limitations and accountability, and know how and when to seek advice from a range of sources, including professional supervision

    iv.   use support networks and professional supervision to manage uncertainty, change and stress in work situations while maintaining resilience in self and others

    v.   handle conflict between others and internally when personal views may conflict with a course of action necessitated by the social work role

    vi.   provide reasoned, informed arguments to challenge unacceptable practices in a responsible manner and raise concerns about wrongdoing in the workplace

    vii.   be open and honest with people if things go wrong

    viii.   understand the difference between theory, research, evidence and expertise and the role of professional judgement.

Use of technology and numerical skills

5.18 Graduates in social work are able to use information and communication technology effectively and appropriately for:

i.   professional communication, data storage and retrieval and information searching
ii. accessing and assimilating information to inform working with people who use services
iii. data analysis to enable effective use of research in practice
iv. enhancing skills in problem-solving
v.   applying numerical skills to financial and budgetary responsibilities
vi. understanding the social impact of technology, including the constraints of confidentiality and an awareness of the impact of the 'digital divide'.

© The Quality Assurance Agency for Higher Education, 2019 http://www.qaa.ac.uk/

References

Abrams, L (2002) *The Making of Modern Woman: Europe 1789–1918.* London: Pearson Education.

Adam, BD (1978) *The Survival of Domination: Inferiorization and Everyday Life.* New York: Elsevier.

Anon (2019) *Safeguarding Children and Young People: Roles and Competencies for Healthcare Staff,* 4th edn. London: The Royal College of Nursing.

Argyris, C (1982) *Reasoning, Learning, and Action: Individual and Organizational.* San Francisco: Jossey-Bass.

Bainbridge, D (2009) *Teenagers: A Natural History.* London: Portobello.

Barter, C, McCarry, M, Berridge, D and Evans, K (2009) *Partner Exploitation and Violence in Teenage Intimate Relationships.* London: NSPCC.

Becker, HS (1966) *Outsiders: Studies in the Sociology of Deviance.* New York: The Free Press.

Bernstein, R (1974) Are we still stereotyping the unmarried mother? In HJ Parad (ed.), *Crisis Intervention: Selected Readings.* New York: Family Service Association of America.

Bourdieu, P (1977) *Outline of a Theory of Practice.* New York: Cambridge University Press.

Bourdieu, P (1984) *Distinction: A Social Critique of the Judgement of Taste.* London: Routledge.

Bourdieu, P (1990) *In Other Words: Essays Towards a Reflexive Sociology.* Cambridge: Polity Press.

Bourdieu, P (1991) *Language and Symbolic Power,* Cambridge: Polity Press.

Bourdieu, P (2003) *Participant Objectivation,* this is the revised text of the Huxley Memorial Lecture, as delivered by Pierre Bourdieu at the Royal Anthropological Institute on 6 December 2000. The final version was prepared and translated from the French by Loïc Wacquant in April 2002. Available at: https://onlinelibrary.wiley.com/doi/abs/10.1111/1467-9655.00150

Bowers-Brown, T (2018) 'It's like if you don't go to uni you fail in life': the relationship between girls' educational choices and the forms of capital. In J Thatcher, N Ingram, C Burke and J Abrahams (eds), *Bourdieu: The Next Generation: The Development of Bourdieu's Intellectual Heritage in Contemporary UK Sociology.* Oxon: Routledge.

British Association of Social Workers (2018) *Professional Capabilities Framework.* Birmingham: BASW. Available at: https://www.basw.co.uk/social-work-training/professional-capabilities-framework-pcf

British Association of Social Workers (2021) *The BASW Code of Ethics for Social Work.* Birmingham: BASW. Available at: https://www.basw.co.uk/system/files/resources/basw_code_of_ethics_-_2021.pdf

British Association of Social Workers (undated) *The Digital Capabilities Statement for Social Work.* Birmingham: BASW. Available at: https://www.basw.co.uk/digital-capabilities-statement-social-workers

Bronfenbrenner, U (1979) *The Ecology of Human Development: Experiments by Nature and Design.* Cambridge: Harvard University Press.

Bronfenbrenner, U (1994) Ecological models of human development. In T Husen and TN Postlethwaite (eds), *International Encyclopaedia of Education,* Vol. 3, 2nd ed. Oxford: Elsevier, pp. 3–44.

Bronfenbrenner, U (ed) (2005) *Making Human Beings Human: Bioecological Perspectives on Human Development.* London: Sage.

Bryant, G, Heard, H and Watson, J (2015) *Measuring Mental Wellbeing in Children and Young People*. London: Public Health England. Available at: https://assets.publishing.service.gov.uk/government/uploads/system/uploads/attachment_data/file/768983/Measuring_mental_wellbeing_in_children_and_young_people.pdf

Butler, J (1996) Professional development: practice as text, reflection as process, and self as locus. *Australian Journal of Education*, 40(3): 265–83.

Calder, MC and Archer, J (2015) *Risk in Child Protection: Assessment Challenges and Frameworks for Practice*. London: Jessica Kingsley.

Child Poverty Action Group (2021) *Child Poverty Facts and Figures: March 2021*. Available at: https://cpag.org.uk/child-poverty/child-poverty-facts-and-figures#footnote1_nbcbrf2

Chisnell, C and Kelly, C (2019) *Safeguarding in Social Work Practice: A Lifespan Approach*. London: Sage/Learning Matters.

Clarke, J (2002) Social problems: sociological perspectives. In M May, R Page and E Brunsdon (eds), *Understanding Social Problems: Issues in Social Policy*. Oxford: Blackwell.

Congress, EP (1994) The use of culturagrams to assess and empower culturally diverse families, *Families in Society*, 75(9): 531–40.

Cotgrove, S (1970) *The Science of Society: An Introduction to Sociology*: London: George Allen and Unwin.

Crossley, S (2018) *Troublemaker: The Construction of 'Troubled Families' as a Social Problem*. Bristol: Policy Press.

Cunliffe, AL (2004) On becoming a critically reflexive practitioner, *Journal of Management Education*, 28(4): 407–26.

Dallos, R and Sapsford, R (1997) Patterns of diversity and lived realities. In J Muncie, M Wetherell, M Langan, R Dallos and A Cochrane (eds), *Understanding the Family*, 2nd edn. London: Sage.

Davies, L and Duckett, N (2019) *Proactive Child Protection and Social Work*, 2nd edn. London: Sage/Learning Matters.

D'Cruz, H, Gillingham, P and Melendez, S (2007) Reflexivity, its meanings and relevance for social work: a critical review of the literature, *British Journal of Social Work*, 37: 73–90.

Dean, H (2019) *Social Policy*, 3rd edn. Cambridge: Polity Press.

Department for Education (2018) *Knowledge and Skills Statement for Child and Family Practitioners*. London: Crown.

Diaz, C (2020) *Decision Making in Child and Family Social Work Perspectives on Children's Participation*. Bristol: Policy Press.

Duncan, S (2007) What's the problem with teenage parents? And what's the problem with policy? *Critical Social Policy*, 27(3): 307–34.

Dykes, C (2019) *Writing Analytical Assessments in Social Work*, 2nd edn. St Albans: Critical Publishing.

Elliott, A (2009) *Contemporary Social Theory: An Introduction*. Abingdon: Routledge.

Elliott, A (2020) *Concepts of Self*, 4th edn. Cambridge: Polity Press.

Ellis-Sloan, K (2014) Teenage mothers, stigma and their 'presentations of self'. *Sociological Research Online*, 19: 1–9.

Evans, T (2011) The other woman and her child: Extra-marital affairs and illegitimacy in twentieth-century Britain, *Women's History Review*, 20(1): 47–65.

Fearnley, R (2012) *Communicating with Children When a Parent Is at the End of Life*. London: Jessica Kingsley.

Fearnley, B (2018) Contemporary young motherhood: experiences of hostility. *Journal of Children's Services*, 13(2): 64–78.

Finch, J (2007) Displaying families. *Sociology*, 41(1): 65–81.

Fink, J (2011) For better or for worse? The dilemmas of unmarried motherhood in mid twentieth century popular British film and fiction. *Women's History Review*, 20(1): 145–60.

Fisher-Borne, M, Cain, JM and Martin, SL (2015) From mastery to accountability: cultural humility as an alternative to cultural competence. *Social Work Education*, 34(2): 165–81. https://doi.org/10.1080/02615479.2014.977244

Flexner, A (1915) Is social work a profession? In *National Conference of Charities and Corrections, Proceedings of the National Conference of Charities and Corrections at the Forty-second Annual Session held in Baltimore, Maryland, May 12–19, 1915*. Chicago: Hildmann.

Fox, CL, Corr, ML, Gadd, D and Butler, I (2014) Young teenagers' experiences of domestic abuse. *Journal of Youth Studies*, 17(4): 510–26.

Freeman-Powell, S (2019) Why 56 black men are posing in hoodies. *BBC News*. Published 20 February 2019. Available at: https://www.bbc.co.uk/news/uk-47298111

Friedman, E and Billick, SB (2015) Unintentional child neglect: literature review and observational study. *Psychiatric Quarterly*, 86(2): 253–9.

Friedman, S and Laurison, D (2020) *The Class Ceiling: Why Is Pays to Be Privileged*. Bristol: Policy Press.

Friedman, S (2018) The limits of capital gains: using bourdieu to understand social mobility into elite occupations. In J Thatcher, N Ingram, C Burke and J Abrahams (eds), *Bourdieu: The Next Generation: The Development of Bourdieu's Intellectual Heritage in Contemporary UK Sociology*. Oxon: Routledge.

Frost, N (2021) *Safeguarding Children and Young People: A Guide for Professionals Working Together*. London: Sage.

Gelles, RJ (1995) *Contemporary Families: A Sociological View*. London: Sage.

Gibbs, G (1988) *Learning by Doing: A Guide to Teaching and Learning Methods, Further Education Unit*. Oxford: Oxford Polytechnic.

Giddens, A (2009) *Sociology*, 6th edn. Cambridge: Polity Press.

Gingerbread (2019) *Single Parents: Facts and Figures: Posted 16 April 2019*. Available at: https://www.gingerbread.org.uk/?s=Single+parents

Goffman, E (1959/1990) *The Presentation of Self in Everyday Life*. London: Penguin.

Gros, L, Debue, N, Lete, J and van de Leemput, C (2020) Video game addiction and emotional states: possible confusion between pleasure and happiness? *Frontier Psychology*. https://doi.org/10.3389/fpsyg.2019.02894

Harris, JC and Kirby, J (2019) *Implementing 'Was Not Brought' in Your Practice: A Tool for Safeguarding Children Who Miss Appointments*. Sheffield Teaching Hospitals, Health Education England, British Dental Association. Available at: https://bda.org/advice/Documents/Was%20Not%20Brought%20implementation%20guide%20AW.pdf

Harris, JC, Sidebotton, P and Welbury, R (2009) *Child Protection and the Dental Team: An Introduction to Safeguarding Children in Dental Practice*. Sheffield: Committee of Postgraduate Dental Deans and Directors (COPEND). Available at: https://bda.org/childprotection/Resources/Documents/Childprotectionandthedentalteam_v1_4_Nov09.pdf

HM Government (2020) *Working Together to Safeguard Children Statutory Framework: Legislation Relevant to Safeguarding and Promoting the Welfare of Children July 2018*. London: HM Government. Avaiablbe at: https://assets.publishing.service.gov.uk/government/uploads/system/uploads/attachment_data/file/942455/Working_together_to_safeguard_children_Statutory_framework_legislation_relevant_to_safeguarding_and_promoting_the_welfare_of_children.pdf

Holden, C (2007) *The Shadow of Marriage: Singleness in England, 1914–60*. Manchester: Manchester University Press.

Home Office (2014) *Multi Agency Working and Information Sharing Project Final Report*. London: Home Office. Available at: https://assets.publishing.service.gov.uk/government/uploads/system/uploads/attachment_data/file/338875/MASH.pdf

Home Office (2020) *Guidance Criminal Exploitation of Children and Vulnerable Adults: County Lines*. Updated 7 February 2020. Available at: https://www.gov.uk/government/publications/criminal-exploitation-of-children-and-vulnerable-adults-county-lines/criminal-exploitation-of-children-and-vulnerable-adults-county-lines

Ingram, R (2013) Emotions, social work practice and supervision: an uneasy alliance? *Journal of Social Work Practice*, 27(1): 5–19.

International Association of Schools of Social Work and International Federation of Social Workers (IFSW) (2014) *Global Definition of Social Work*. Rheinfelden: International Association Federation of Social Workers. Available at: https://www.ifsw.org/what-is-social-work/global-definition-of-social-work/

Jamieson, L (2005) Boundaries of intimacy. In L McKie and S Cunningham-Burley (eds), *Families in Society: Boundaries and Relationships*. Bristol: Policy Press.

Jay, A (2014) *Independent Inquiry into Child Sexual Exploitation in Rotherham (1997–2013)*. Available at: https://www.rotherham.gov.uk/downloads/download/31/independent-inquiry-into-child-sexual-exploitation-in-rotherham-1997–2013

Johns, R (2020) *Using the Law in Social Work*, 8th edn. London: Sage/Learning Matters.

Johnson, M (2013) *Evaluating Culture: Well-Bing, Institutions and Circumstance*. Basingstoke: Palgrave MacMillan.

Jones, C, Whitfield, C, Seymour, J and Hayter, M (2019) 'Other girls': a qualitative exploration of teenage mothers' views on teen pregnancy, contemporaries. *Sexuality and Culture*, 23: 760–73.

Jordan, B (1984) *Invitation to Social Work*. Oxford: Blackwell.

Keeling, J and Goosey, D (2020) *Safeguarding Across the Life Span*. London: Sage.

Keesing, RM (1976) *Cultural Anthropology: A Contemporary Perspective*. New York: Hunt Rinehart and Winston.

Killick, C and Taylor, B (2020) *Assessment, Risk and Decision Making in Social Work: An Introduction*. London: Sage/Learning Matters.

Kirby, J and Harris, JC (2019) Development and evaluation of a 'was not brought' pathway: a team approach to managing children's missed dental appointments. *British Dental Journal*, 227: 291–7.

Kolb, D (1984) *Experiential Learning: Experience as the Source of Learning and Development*. Englewood Cliffs, NJ: Prentice-Hall.

Kondrat, DC (2020) Solution-focused practice. In B Teater (ed.), *An Introduction to Applying Social Work Theories and Methods*, 2nd edn. Maidenhead: Open University Press.

Kondrat, DC (2020) Strengths based perspective. In B Teater (ed.), *An Introduction to Applying Social Work Theories and Methods*, 2nd edn. Maidenhead: Open University Press.

Koprowska, J (2020) *Communication and Interpersonal Skills in Social Work*. London: Sage/Learning Matters.

Kulkarni, S (2007) Romance narrative, feminine ideals, and developmental detours for yong mothers. *Journal of Women and Social Work*, 22(1): 9–22.

Lemert, EM (1972) *Human Deviance, Social Problems and Social Control*, 2nd edn. London: Prentice-Hill International.

Link, BG and Phelan, JC (2006) Stigma and its public health implications. *The Lancet*, 367: 528–9.

Loft, P (2020) *The Troubled Families Programme (England)*. Briefing Paper Number 07585, 27 November 2020. London: House of Commons. Available at: https://researchbriefings.files.parliament.uk/documents/CBP-7585/CBP-7585.pdf

Lynch, M (2000) Against reflexivity as an academic virtue and source of privileged knowledge. *Theory, Culture, and Society*, 17(3): 26–54.

Macvarish, J (2010) Understanding the significance of the teenage mother in contemporary parenting culture. *Sociological Research Online*, 15(4). https://journals.sagepub.com/doi/10.5153/sro.2238

Mantell, A and Scragg, T (eds) (2019) *Reflective Practice in Social Work*, 5th edn. London: Sage/ Learning Matters.

Mckenzie, L (2018) Narrative, ethnography and class inequality: taking Bourdieu into a British Council Estate. In J Thatcher, N Ingram, C Burke and J Abrahams (eds), *Bourdieu: The Next Generation: The Development of Bourdieu's Intellectual Heritage in Contemporary UK Sociology*. Oxon: Routledge.

McKie, L and Callan, S (2012) *Understanding Families: A Global Perspective*. London: Sage.

McRobbie, A (2009) *The Aftermath of Feminism: Gender, Culture and Social Change*. London: Sage.

McSherry, W, Rodriguez, A and Smith, J (2020) Moral, spiritual and existential development. In J Parker and S Ashencaen Crabtree (eds), *Human Growth and Development in Children and Young People*. Bristol: Policy Press.

Melrose, M (2013) Twenty-first century party people: young people and sexual exploitation in the new millennium. *Child Abuse Review*, 22: 155–68.

Moran-Ellis, J (2010) Reflections on sociology of childhood in the UK. *Current Sociology*, 58(2): 186–205.

Morgan, DHJ (1996) *Family Connections: An Introduction to Family Studies*. Cambridge: Polity Press.

Morgan, DHG (2011) Locating 'family practices'. *Sociological Research Online*, 16(4): 14.

Morgan, DHJ (2013) *Rethinking Family Practices*. Basingstoke: Palgrave Macmillan.

Muncie, J and Sapsford, R (1997) Issues in the study of 'the family'. In J Muncie, M Wetherell, M Langan, R Dallos and A Cochrane (eds), *Understanding the Family*, 2nd edn. London: Sage.

Munro, ER and Zonouzi, M with Fountain, R, Harris, J, Vale, D and a Group of Disabled Parents (2018) *Re-imagining Social Care Services in Co-production with Disabled Parents*. Bedford: University of Bedford.

Murray, C (1990) *The Emerging British Underclass*. London: Institute of Economic Affairs.

Neill-Weston, F and Morgan, M (2017) Teenage childbearing: young sole mothers challenge the stereotypes. *Kōtuitui: New Zealand Journal of Social Sciences*, 12(2): 179–91.

Nobbs, J, Hine, B and Flemming, M (1980) *Sociology*. Basingstoke: MacMillan.

Northern Ireland Social Care Council (2019) *Standards of Conduct and Practice for Social Workers*, Belfast: Northern Ireland Social Care Council. Available at: https://niscc.info/app/ uploads/2020/09/standards-of-conduct-and-practice-for-social-workers-2019.pdf

Oakley, A (1974) *The Sociology of Housework*. London: Martin Robertson & Company.

Oakley, A (1976) *Housewife*. Middlesex: Penguin Books.

Office for National Statistics (2020) *Child Abuse Extent and Nature. England and Wales: Year Ending March 2019*. Available at: https://www.ons.gov.uk/peoplepopulationandcommunity/ crimeandjustice/bulletins/childabuseinenglandandwales/march2020

Oko, J (2011) *Understanding and Using Theory in Social Work*. London: Sage/Learning Matters.

Parker, J (2020) Critical perspectives. In J Parker and S Ashencaen Crabtree (eds), *Human Growth and Development in Children and Young People*. Bristol: Policy Press.

Parker, J. (2021) *Social Work Practice: Assessment, Planning, Intervention and Review*, 6th edn. London: Sage/Learning Matters.

Parker, J. and Ashencaen Crabtree, S. (2018), *Social Work with Disadvantaged and Marginalised People*. London: Sage/Learning Matters.

Parker, J and Ashencaen Crabtree, S (eds) (2020), *Human Growth and Development in Children and Young People*. Bristol: Policy Press.

Parker, J and Doel, M (2013) Professional social work and social work identity. In J Parker and M Doel (eds), *Professional Social Work*. London: Sage/Learning Matters.

Parker, J and Finch, J (2020) The history and context of contemporary social work (including global social work). In J Parker (ed.), *Introducing Social Work*. London: Sage/Learning Matters.

Penakalapati, G, Swarthout, J, Delahoy, MJ, McAliley, L, Wodnik, B, Levy, K and Freeman, MC (2017) Exposure to animal feces and human health: a systematic review and proposed research priorities. *Environmental Science and Technology*, 51(20): 11537–52.

Philips, CR (2014) 'Seeing the child' beyond the literal: considering dance choreography and the body in child welfare and protection. *The British Journal of Social Work*, 44(8): 2254–71.

Pitchforth, J, Fahy, K, Ford, T, Wolpert, M, Viner, RM, Hargreaves, DS (2019) Mental health and well-being trends among children and young people in the UK, 1995–2014: analysis of repeated cross-sectional national health surveys, *Psychological Medicine*, 49: 1275–85.

Public Health England (2019) *A Framework for Supporting Teenage Mothers and Young Fathers*. London: Public Health England.

Quality Assurance Agency (QAA) (2019) *Subject Statement Social Work*. Gloucester: Quality Assurance Agency for Higher Education.

Saleeby, D (2009) *The Strengths Perspective in Social Work Practice*, 5th edn. Boston, MA: Allyn and Bacon.

Schön, DA (1983) *The Reflective Practitioner: How Professions Think in Action*. London: Temple Smith.

Schur, EM (1984) *Labelling Women Deviant, Gender, Stigma, and Social Control*. New York: McGraw-hill Publishing Company.

Scottish Social Services Council (SSSC) (2016) *Codes of Practice for Social Service Workers and Employers*. Dundee: SSSC. file: https://www.sssc.uk.com/the-scottishsocial-servicescouncil/sssccodes-of-practice/

Senge, P, Roberts, C, Ross, R, Smith, B and Kleiner, A (1994) *The Fifth Discipline Fieldbook*. New York: Bantam Doubleday Dell.

Shelter (2019) *A Child Becomes Homeless in Britain Every Eight Minutes*. Available at: https://england.shelter.org.uk/media/press_release/a_child_becomes_homeless_in_britain_every_eight_minutes

Shulman, LS (2005) Signature pedagogies in the professions. *Daedalus*, 134(3): 52–9.

Social Care Wales (2017) *Code of Professional Practice for Social Care*. Cardiff: Social Care Wales. Available at: https://socialcare.wales/cms_assets/file-uploads/Code-of-Professional-Practice-for-Social-Care-web-version.pdf

Social Exclusion Unit (1999) *Teenage Pregnancy*. London: The Stationary Office.

Social Work England (2020) *Guidance on the Professional Standards*. Sheffield: Social Work England. Available at: https://www.socialworkengland.org.uk/standards/professional-standards-guidance/

Social Work England (2020) *Professional Standards*. Sheffield: Social Work England. Available at: https://www.socialworkengland.org.uk/media/1640/1227_socialworkengland_standards_prof_standards_final-aw.pdf

Social Workers Regulations (2018) *PART 6: Restrictions on Practice, Protected Titles and Offences: Section 28. Carrying Out Social Work in England and Use of Title*. Available at: https://www.legislation.gov.uk/uksi/2018/893/regulation/28

Spillman, L (2020) *What Is Cultural Sociology*. Cambridge: Polity Press.

Stapleton, H (2010) *Surviving Teenage Motherhood: Myths and Realities*. Basingstoke: Palgrave Macmillan.

Taylor, A (2017) Social work and digitalisation: bridging the knowledge gaps. *Social Work Education*, 36(8): 869–79.

Teater, B (2020) *An Introduction to Applying Social Work Theories and Methods*, 3rd edn. Maidenhead: Open University Press.

Thatcher, J, Ingram, N, Burke, C and Abrahams, J (eds) (2018) *Bourdieu: The Next Generation: The Development of Bourdieu's Intellectual Heritage in Contemporary UK Sociology*. Oxon: Routledge.

The Social Mobility Commission (2019) *State of the Nation 2018–19: Social Mobility in Great Britain*. London: The Social Mobility Commission.

Thornicroft, G, Rose, D, Kassam, A and Sartorius, N (2007) Stigma: ignorance, prejudice or discrimination? *The British Journal of Psychiatry*, 190: 192–3.

Timms, N and Timms, R (1977) *Perspectives in Social Work*. Oxon: Routledge and Kegan Paul.

Trevithick, P (2012) *Social Work Skills and Knowledge: A Practice Handbook*, 3rd edn. Maidenhead: Open University Press.

UK Rehab (undated) *Gaming Addiction Explained*. Available at: https://www.uk-rehab.com/behavioural-addictions/gaming/

United Nations High Commissioner for Refugees (UNHCR) (Undated) *Convention and Protocol Relating to the Status of Refugees*. Available at: https://www.unhcr.org/3b66c2aa10.html

Vizard, T, Sadler, K, Ford, T, Newlove-Delgado, T, McManus, S, Marcheselli, F, Davis, J, Williams, T, Leach, C, Mandalia, D and Cartwright, C (2020) Mental health of children and young people in England. *NHS Digital*. Available at: https://digital.nhs.uk/data-and-information/publications/statistical/mental-health-of-children-and-young-people-in-england/2020-wave-1-follow-up

Walker, J and Horner, H (2020) *Social Work and Human Development*, 6th edn. London: Sage/Learning Matters.

Walker, J, Crawford, K and Parker, J (2008) *Practice Education in Social Work: A Handbook for Practice Researchers, Assessors and Educators*. Exeter: Learning Matters.

Walsh, JC and Mason, W (2018) Walking the walk: changing familial forms, government policy and social work practice. *Social Policy and Society*, 17(4): 603–18. https://doi.org/10.1017/S1474746418000209

Wastell, D and White, S (2017) *Blinded by Science: The Social Implications of Epigenetics and Neuroscience*. Bristol: Policy Press.

Welshman, J (2007) *From Transmitted Deprivation to Social Exclusion: Policy, Poverty and Parenting*. Bristol: Policy Press.

Welshman, J (2013) *Underclass*, 2nd edn. London: Bloomsbury.

Wenham (2016) "I know I'm a good mum – no one can tell me different." Young mothers negotiating a stigmatised identity through time. *Families, Relationships and Societies*, 5(1): 127–44.

Williams, F (2004) *Rethinking Families*. London: Calouste Gulbenkian Foundation.

Wills, J, Whittaker, A, Rickard, W and Felix, C (2017) Troubled, troubling or in trouble: the stories of 'troubled families'. *British Journal of Social Work*, 47: 989–1006.

Wilson, H and Huntington, A (2005) Deviant (m)others: the construction of teenagers in contemporary discourse. *Journal of Social Policy*, 35(1): 59–76.

Witkin, SL (2017) *Transforming Social Work*. London: Palgrave.

Wonnacott, J (2012) *Mastering Social Work Supervision*. London: Jessica Kingsley.

Index